COWMEN AND RUSTLERS

A Story of the Wyoming Cattle Ranges

EDWARD S. ELLIS

1st WORLD
LIBRARY
Literary Society

Cowmen and Rustlers

Edward S. Ellis

© 1st World Library, 2007
PO Box 2211
Fairfield, IA 52556
www.1stworldlibrary.com
First Edition

LCCN: 2007930739

Softcover ISBN: 978-1-4218-4814-3
Hardcover ISBN: 978-1-4218-4717-7
eBook ISBN: 978-1-4218-4911-9

Purchase *"Cowmen and Rustlers"*
as a traditional bound book at:
www.1stWorldLibrary.com/purchase.asp?ISBN=978-1-4218-4814-3

1st World Library is a literary, educational organization
dedicated to:

- Creating a free internet library of downloadable ebooks

- Hosting writing competitions and offering book publishing
  scholarships.

Interested in more 1st World Library books? contact:
literacy@1stworldlibrary.com
Check us out at: www.1stworldlibrary.com

1st World Library Literary Society

Giving Back to the World

"If you want to work on the core problem, it's early school literacy."

- James Barksdale, former CEO of Netscape

"No skill is more crucial to the future of a child, or to a democratic and prosperous society, than literacy."

- Los Angeles Times

"Literacy... means far more than learning how to read and write... The aim is to transmit... knowledge and promote social participation."

- UNESCO

"Literacy is not a luxury, it is a right and a responsibility. If our world is to meet the challenges of the twenty-first century we must harness the energy and creativity of all our citizens."

- President Bill Clinton

"Parents should be encouraged to read to their children, and teachers should be equipped with all available techniques for teaching literacy, so the varying needs and capacities of individual kids can be taken into account."

- Hugh Mackay

CONTENTS

CHAPTER I

A MERRY GROUP

The Whitney household, in the western part of Maine, was filled with sunshine, merriment and delight, on a certain winter evening a few years ago.

There was the quiet, thoughtful mother, now past her prime, but with many traces of the beauty and refinement that made her the belle of the little country town until Hugh Whitney, the strong-bearded soldier, who had entered the war as private and emerged therefrom with several wounds and with the eagles of a colonel on his shoulder, carried her away from all admirers and made her his bride.

Hugh had been absent a couple of weeks in Montana and Wyoming, whither he was drawn by a yearning of many years' standing to engage in the cattle business. He had received some tuition as a cowboy on the Llano Estacada, and the taste there acquired of the free, wild life, supplemented, doubtless, by his experience during the war, was held in restraint for a time only by his marriage.

The absence of the father was the only element lacking to make the household one of the happiest in that section of Maine; but the letter just received from him was so cheerful and affectionate that it added to the enjoyment of the family.

The two principal factors in this jollity were the twins and only children, Fred and Jennie, seventeen on their last birthday, each the picture of health, bounding spirits, love and devotion to their parents and to one another. They had been the life of the sleighing-parties and social gatherings, where the beauty of the budding Jennie attracted as much admiration as did that of her mother a score of years before, but the girl was too young to care for any of the ardent swains who were ready to wrangle for the privilege of a smile or encouraging word. Like a good and true daughter she had no secrets from her mother, and when that excellent parent said, with a meaning smile, "Wait a few years, Jennie," the girl willingly promised to do as she wished in that as in every other respect.

Fred was home for the Christmas holidays, and brought with him Monteith Sterry, one year his senior. Sterry lived in Boston, where he and Fred Whitney were classmates and warm friends. Young Whitney had spent several Sundays with Sterry, and the latter finally accepted the invitation to visit him at his home down in Maine.

These two young men, materially aided by Jennie, speedily turned the house topsy-turvy. There was no resisting their overrunning spirits, though now and then the mother ventured on a mild protest, but the smile which always accompanied the gentle reproof betrayed the truth, that she was as happy as they in their merriment, with which she would not have interfered for the world.

That night the full, round moon shone from an unclouded sky, and the air was crisp and clear. There was not much snow on the ground, and the ice on the little river at the rear of the house was as smooth as a polished window-pane. For

Edward S. Ellis

nearly two score miles this current, which eventually found its way into the Penobscot, wound through the leafless woods, past an occasional opening, where, perhaps, the humble cabin of some backwoodsman stood.

It was an ideal skating rink, and the particular overflow of spirits on that evening was due to the agreement that it was to be devoted to the exhilarating amusement.

"We will leave the house at 8 o'clock," said Fred at the supper table, "and skate to the mouth of Wild Man's Creek and back."

"How far is that?" inquired Monteith Sterry.

"About ten miles."

Pretty Jennie's face took on a contemptuous expression.

"Not a bit more; we shall be only fairly started when we must turn back."

"Well, where do you want to go, sister?"

"We shouldn't think of stopping until we reach Wolf Glen."

"And may I inquire the distance to that spot?" asked Sterry again.

"Barely five miles beyond Wild Man's Creek," said she.

Those were not the young men to take a "dare" from a girl like her. It will be admitted that thirty miles is a pretty good spurt for a skater, but the conditions could not have been more favourable.

"It's agreed, then," remarked Sterry, "that we will go to Wolf Glen, and then, and then—"

"And then what?" demanded Jennie, turning toward him.

"Why not keep on to Boston and call on my folks?"

"If you will furnish the ice we will do so."

"I couldn't guarantee ice all the way, but we can travel by other means between the points, using our skates as the chance offers."

"Or do as that explorer who is to set out in search of the north pole—have a combination skate and boat, so when fairly going we can keep straight on."

"I will consent to that arrangement on one condition," interposed the mother, so seriously that all eyes were turned wonderingly upon her.

"What is that?"

"That you return before the morrow."

The countenances became grave, and turning to Sterry, on her right, Jennie asked, in a low voice:

"Is it safe to promise that?"

"Hardly. Let us leave the scheme until we have time in which fully to consider it."

"You will start, as I understand, at eight," remarked the mother, speaking now in earnest. "You can readily reach Wolf Glen within a couple of hours. There you will rest a

Edward S. Ellis

while and return as you choose. So I will expect you at midnight."

"Unless something happens to prevent."

The words of Monteith Sterry were uttered jestingly, but they caused a pang to the affectionate parent as she asked:

"What could happen, Monteith?"

Fred took it upon himself to reply promptly:

"Nothing at all."

"Is the ice firm and strong?"

"It will bear a locomotive; I never saw it finer; the winter has not been so severe as some we have known, but it has got there all the same; Maine can furnish the Union with all the ice she will want next summer."

"There may be air-holes."

"None that we cannot see; they are few and do not amount to anything."

Here Sterry spoke with mock gravity.

"The name, Wolf Glen, is ominous."

"We have wolves and bears and other big game in this part of the State, but not nearly as many as formerly. It hardly pays to hunt them."

"I hope we shall meet a few bears or wolves," said Jennie, with her light laugh.

"And why?" demanded the shocked mother.

"I would like a race with them; wouldn't it be fun!"

"Yes," replied Sterry, "provided we could outskate them."

"I never knew that wild animals skate."

"They can travel fast when they take it into their heads to turn hunter. I suppose many of the bears are hibernating, but the wolves—if there are any waiting for us—will be wide awake and may give us the roughest kind of sport."

Fred Whitney knew his mother better than did his friend and understood the expression on her face. So did Jennie, and the couple had such sport of their Boston visitor that the cloud quickly vanished and Monteith felt a trifle humiliated at his exhibition of what might be considered timidity. Nevertheless he quietly slipped his loaded revolver in the outer pocket of his heavy coat just before starting and when no one was watching him.

Precisely at eight o'clock the three friends, warmly and conveniently clad, with their keen-edged skates securely fastened, glided gracefully up-stream, the mother standing on the porch of her home and watching the figures as they vanished in the moonlight.

She was smiling, but in her heart was a misgiving such as she had not felt before, when her children were starting off for an evening's enjoyment. The minute they were beyond sight she sighed, and, turning about, resumed her seat by the table in the centre of the sitting-room, where, as the lamplight fell upon her pale face, she strove to drive away the disquieting thoughts that would not leave her.

Edward S. Ellis

It was a pleasing sight as the three young people, the picture of life, health and joyous spirits, side by side, laughing, jesting, and with never a thought of danger, moved out to the middle of the river and then sped toward its source, with the easy, beautiful movement which in the accomplished skater is the ideal of grace. The motion seemingly was attended with no effort, and could be maintained for hours with little fatigue.

The small river, to which allusion has been made, was one hundred yards in width at the point where they passed out upon its surface. This width naturally decreased as they ascended, but the decrease was so gradual that at Wolf Glen, fifteen miles away, the breadth was fully three-fourths of the width opposite the Whitney home. Occasionally, too, the channel widened to double or triple its usual extent, but those places were few in number, and did not continue long. They marked a shallowing of the current and suggested in appearance a lake.

There were other spots where this tributary itself received others. Sometimes the open space would show on the right, and further on another on the left indicated where a creek debouched into the stream, in its search for the ocean, the great depository of most of the rivers of the globe.

The trees, denuded of vegetation, projected their bare limbs into the crystalline air, and here and there, where they leaned over the banks, were thrown in relief against the moonlit sky beyond. The moon itself was nearly in the zenith, and the reflected gleam from the glassy surface made the light almost like that of day. Along the shore, however, the shadows were so gloomy and threatening that Monteith Sterry more than once gave a slight shudder and reached his mittened hand down to his side to make sure his weapon was in place.

The course was sinuous from the beginning, winding in and out so continuously that the length of the stream must have been double that of the straight line extending over the same course. Some of these turnings were abrupt, and there were long, sweeping curves with a view extending several hundred yards.

They were spinning around one of these, when Sterry uttered an exclamation:

"I'm disappointed!"

"Why?" inquired Jennie, at his elbow.

"I had just wrought myself up to the fancy that we were pioneers, the first people of our race to enter this primeval wilderness, when lo!"

He extended his arm up-stream and to the right, where a star-like twinkle showed that a dwelling stood, or some parties had kindled a camp-fire.

"Quance, an old fisherman and hunter, lives, there," explained Fred, "as I believe he has done for fifty years."

"Would you like to make a call on him?" asked Jennie.

"I have no desire to do so; I enjoy this sport better than to sit by the fire and listen to the most entertaining hunter. Isn't that he?"

The cabin was several rods from the shore, the space in front being clear of trees and affording an unobstructed view of the little log structure, with its single door and window in front, and the stone chimney from which the smoke was ascending. Half-way between the cabin and the stream, and in the path connecting the two, stood a man with folded arms looking at them. He was so motionless that he suggested a stump, but the bright moonlight left no doubt of his identity.

"Holloa, Quance!" shouted Fred, slightly slackening his speed and curving in toward shore.

The old man made no reply. Then Jennie's musical voice rang out on the frosty air, but still the hunter gave no sign that he knew he had been addressed. He did not move an arm nor stir.

"I wonder whether he hasn't frozen stiff in that position," remarked Sterry. "He may have been caught in the first snap several weeks ago and has been acting ever since as his own monument."

At the moment of shooting out of sight around the curve the three glanced back. The old fellow was there, just as they saw him at first. They even fancied he had not so much as turned his head while they were passing, but was still gazing at the bank opposite him, or, what was more likely, peering sideways without shifting his head to any extent.

The occurrence, however, was too slight to cause a second thought.

They were now fairly under way, as may be said, being more than a mile from their starting-point. They were proceeding swiftly but easily, ready to decrease or increase their speed at a moment's notice. Sometimes they were nigh enough to touch each other's hands, and again they separated, one going far to the right, the other to the left, while the third kept near the middle of the stream. Then two would swerve toward shore, or perhaps it was all three, and again it was Jennie who kept the farthest from land, or perhaps a fancy led her to skim so close that some of the overhanging limbs brushed her face.

"Look out; there's an air-hole!" called the brother, at the moment the three reunited after one of these excursions.

"What of it!" was her demand, and instead of shooting to the right or left, she kept straight on toward the open space.

"Don't try to jump it!" cautioned Sterry, suspecting her purpose; "it's too wide."

"No doubt it is for you."

The daring words were on her lips, when she rose slightly in the air and skimmed as gracefully as a bird across the space of clear water. She came down seemingly without jar, with the bright blades of steel ringing over the crystal surface, and without having fallen a foot to the rear of her companions.

"That was foolish," said her brother, reprovingly; "suppose the ice had given away when you struck it again?"

"What's the use of supposing what could not take place?"

"The air-hole might have been wider than you suppose."

"How could that be when it was in plain sight? If it had been wider, why I would have jumped further, or turned aside like my two gallant escorts. Stick to me and I'll take care of you."

There was no dashing the spirits of the girl, and Sterry broke into laughter, wondering how it would be with her if actual danger did present itself.

Occasionally the happy ones indulged in snatches of song

Edward S. Ellis

and fancy skating, gliding around each other in bewildering and graceful curves. The three were experts, as are nearly all people in that section of the Union. Any one watching their exhibitions of skill and knowing the anxiety of the mother at home would have wondered why she should feel any misgiving concerning them.

True, there were wild animals in the forests, and at this season of the year, when pressed by hunger, they would attack persons if opportunity presented; but could the fleetest outspeed any one of those three, if he or she chose to put forth the utmost strength and skill possessed?

"Look!"

It was Jennie who uttered the exclamation, and there was good cause for it. She was slightly in advance, and was rounding another of the turns of the stream, when she caught sight of a huge black bear, who, instead of staying in some hollow tree or cave, sucking his paw the winter through, was lumbering over the ice in the same direction with themselves.

He was near the middle of the frozen current, so that it was prudent for them to turn to the right or left, and was proceeding at an easy pace, as if he was out for a midnight stroll, while he thought over matters. Though one of the stupidest of animals, he was quick to hear the noise behind him and looked back to learn what it meant.

CHAPTER II

A WARNING FROM THE WOODS

Monteith Sterry began drawing the mitten from his right hand with the intention of using his revolver on the bear, when he checked himself with the thought:

"Better to wait until I need it; the most of this excursion is still before us."

The lumbering brute came to a stop, with his huge head turned, and surveyed the approaching skaters. Had they attempted to flee, or had they come to a halt, probably he would have started after them. As it was he swung half-way round, so that his side was exposed. He offered a fine target for Sterry's weapon, but the young man still refrained from using it.

"It isn't well to go too near him," remarked Fred Whitney, seizing the arm of his sister and drawing her toward the shore on the left.

"I don't mean to," replied the bright-witted girl, "but if we turn away from him too soon he will be able to head us off; he mustn't suspect what we intend to do."

"There's sense in that," remarked Sterry, "but don't wait too long."

The three were skating close together, with their eyes on the big creature, who was watching them sharply.

"Now!" called Fred, in a low, quick voice.

He had not loosened his grip of his sister's arm, so that when he made the turn she was forced to follow him. The moment was well chosen, and the three swung to one side as if all were controlled by the single impulse.

Bruin must have been astonished; for, while waiting for his supper to drop into his arms, he saw it leaving him. With an angry growl he began moving toward the laughing party.

The tinge of anxiety which Fred Whitney felt lasted but a moment. He saw that they could skate faster than the bear could travel; and, had it been otherwise, no cause for fear would have existed, for, with the power to turn like a flash, it would have been the easiest thing in the world to elude the efforts of the animal to seize them.

They expected pursuit, and it looked for a minute as if they were not to be disappointed. The animal headed in their direction with no inconsiderable speed, but, with more intelligence than his kind generally display, he abruptly stopped, turned aside, and disappeared in the wood before it could be said the race had really begun.

Jennie was the most disappointed of the three, for she had counted upon an adventure worth the telling, and here it was nipped in the bud. She expressed her regret.

"There's no helping it," said Monteith, "for I can think of no inducement that will bring him back; but we have a good many miles before us, and it isn't likely that he's the only bear in this part of Maine."

"There's some consolation in that," she replied, leading the way back toward the middle of the course; "if we see another, don't be so abrupt with him."

The stream now broadened to nearly three times its ordinary extent, so that it looked as if they were gliding over the bosom of some lake lagoon instead of a small river. At the widest portion, and from the furthest point on the right, twinkled a second light, so far back among the trees that the structure from whence it came was out of sight. They gave it little attention and kept on.

Sterry took out his watch. The moonlight was so strong that he saw the figures plainly. It lacked a few minutes of nine.

"And yonder is the mouth of Wild Man's Creek," said Fred; "we have made pretty good speed."

"Nothing to boast of," replied Jennie; "if it were not for fear of distressing mother, I would insist that we go ten or fifteen miles further before turning back."

Since plenty of time was at command, they continued their easy pace, passing over several long and comparatively straight stretches of frozen water, around sharp bends, beyond another expansion of the stream, in front of a couple of natural openings, and finally, while it lacked considerable of ten o'clock, they rounded to in front of a mass of gray towering rocks on the right bank of the stream, and, skating close into shore, sat down on a bowlder which obtruded several feet above the ice.

They were at the extremity of their excursion. These collective rocks bore the name of Wolf Glen, the legend being that at some time in the past a horde of wolves made their headquarters there, and, when the winters were unusually severe, held the surrounding country in what might be called a reign of terror. They had not yet wholly disappeared, but little fear of them was felt.

The friends could not be called tired, though, after skating fifteen miles, the rest on the stone was grateful.

They sat for half an hour chatting, laughing, and as merry as when they started from home. The sky was still unclouded, but the moon had passed beyond the zenith. A wall of shadow was thrown out from one of the banks, except for occasional short distances, where the course of the stream was directly toward or from the orb.

When Sterry again glanced at his watch it was a few minutes past ten. They had rested longer than any one suspected.

"Mother won't look for us before midnight," remarked Fred, "and we can easily make it in that time."

"She was so anxious," said the sister, who, despite her light-heartedness, was more thoughtful than her brother, "that I would like to please her by getting back sooner than she expects."

"We have only to keep up this pace to do it," said Monteith, "for we have been resting fully a half hour—"

He paused abruptly. From some point in the wintry wilderness came a dismal, resounding wail, apparently a mile distant.

"What is that?" asked Monteith, less accustomed to the Maine woods than his companions.

"It is the cry of a wolf," replied Fred; "I have heard it many times when hunting alone or with father."

"It isn't the most cheerful voice of the night," commented the young Bostonian, who, as yet never dreamed of connecting it with any peril to themselves. And then he sang:

> Yes, the war whoop of the Indian may produce a pleasant thrill
> When mellowed by the distance that one feels increasing still;
> And the shrilling of the whistle from the engine's brazen snout
> May have minor tones of music, though I never found it out.

The verse was hardly finished when the howl was repeated.

"It is hard to tell from what point it comes," observed Fred, "but I think it is on the right shore as we go back."

"Do you imagine it is far from the river?" inquired Monteith.

"I think not, but I may be mistaken."

"I am quite sure Fred is right," said his sister; "and, more than that, that particular wolf isn't a great way off. I wonder whether he has scented our trail?"

Before any comment could be made upon this remark, a second, third, fourth, and fully a half-dozen additional howls rang through the forest arches. They came from the left shore, and apparently were about as far off as the cry first heard.

Edward S. Ellis

"They are answers," said Fred, in a low voice, in which his companions detected a slight tremor.

It was at this moment that the first fear thrilled all three. The cries might mean nothing, but more likely they meant a good deal. The wolf is one of the fiercest of American wild animals when suffering from hunger, though a coward at other times, and a horde of them are capable of attacking the most formidable denizens of the woods.

The fact that they were between the skaters and home, and at no great distance from the course they must follow to reach there, was cause for fear. It was almost certain that in some way the keen-scented creatures had learned there was game afoot that night for them, and they were signalling to each other to gather for the feast.

Fred and Monteith were not specially frightened on their own account, for, if the worst should come, they could take to the trees and wait for help. They might make a sturdy fight, and perhaps, with anything like a show, could get away from them without taking to such a refuge.

But it was the presence of Jennie that caused the most misgiving. True, she was as swift and skilful a skater as either, but that of itself was not likely to save her.

But she was the coolest of all, now that the danger assumed a reality.

The lightness and gayety that had marked the three from the moment of leaving home had gone. They were thoughtful, the very opposite in their mood to that of a few minutes before.

"I wish I had brought my pistol," said Fred.

"I have mine," observed Monteith; "a good Smith & Wesson, and each of the five chambers is loaded."

"Thank fortune for that; have you any extra cartridges?"

"Not one."

"Your pistol may be the means of saving us."

"Why do you speak that way?" asked Jennie; "I never knew you were scared so easily."

"I am sorry you are with us, sister; my alarm is on your account."

"I do not see why I am not as safe as either of you; neither can skate faster than I."

"If we are to escape by that means, your chances are as good as ours; but those creatures have a fearful advantage over us, because we must run the gauntlet."

"We are not so certain of that; if we hasten, we may pass the danger-point before they discover us."

For the first time since leaving home the three did their best. Separated from each other by just enough space to give play to the limbs, they sped down the icy river with the fleetness of the hurricane, their movements almost the perfect counterpart of each other.

First on the right foot, they shot well toward the shore on that side, then bending gracefully to the left, the weight was thrown on that limb, the impetus being imparted to the body without any apparent effort, after the manner of a master of the skater's art. These, sweeping forward, were many rods in length, the polished steel frequently giving out a metallic ring as it struck the flinty ice. Now and then, too, a resounding creak sped past, and might have alarmed them had they not understood its nature. It indicated no weakness of the frozen surface, but was caused by the settling of the crystal floor as the water flowed beneath.

For a few minutes these were the only noises that broke the impressive stillness. The three had begun to hope that the ominous sounds would be heard no more, and that the wolves were too far from the river to discover them until beyond reach.

If they could once place themselves below the animals they need not fear, for they could readily distance them. Should the speed of the pursuers become dangerous, a sharp turn or change in the course would throw them off and give the fugitives an advantage that would last for a long time. But they dreaded the appearance of a whole pack of the brutes in front, thus shutting off their line of flight homeward. True, in that case they could turn about and flee up stream, but the risk of encountering others attracted by the cries would be great, and perhaps leave their only recourse to a flight into the woods.

The thoughts of each turned to the nearest hunter's cabin, although it was several miles distant, and probably beyond reach.

It was strange that, having emitted so many signals, the wolves should become suddenly quiescent.

No one spoke, but as they glided swiftly forward they peered along the gleaming surface in search of that which they dreaded to see.

They approached one of those long, sweeping bends to which allusion has been made. Jennie had already proven that neither of her companions could outspeed her. They were doing their utmost, but she easily held her own with less effort than they showed.

In truth, she was slightly in advance as they began following the curve of the river, her head, like each of the others, bent forward, to see whither they were going.

"They are there!"

It was she who uttered the exclamation which sent a thrill through both. They asked for no explanation, for none was needed, and an instant later they were at her side, she slightly slackening her pace.

The sight, while alarming, was not all that Fred and Monteith anticipated.

Three or four gaunt animals were trotting along the ice near the left shore, but no others were visible.

"Keep in the middle while I take a turn that way," said Monteith, sheering in the direction named.

Brother and sister did not read the meaning of this course, nor could they detect its wisdom. But they obeyed without question.

Young Sterry hoped by making what might look like an attack upon the famishing beasts to scare them off for a few minutes, during which the three, and especially Jennie, could reach a point below them. With the brutes thus thrown in the rear, it might be said the danger would be over.

Edward S. Ellis

Now, as every one knows, the wolf is a sneak, and generally will run from a child if it presents a bold front; but the animal becomes very dangerous when pressed by hunger.

Monteith Sterry's reception was altogether different from what he anticipated. When the half-dozen wolves saw him speeding toward them they stopped their trotting, and, like the bear, looked around, as not understanding what it meant.

"Confound them! Why don't they take to the woods?" he muttered. He had removed the mitten from his right hand, which grasped his revolver. "This isn't according to Hoyle."

He shied a little to the right, with a view of preventing a collision with the creatures, and the moment he was close enough, let fly with one chamber at the nearest.

Accidentally he nipped the wolf, which emitted a yelping bark, leaped several feet in the air, then limped into the woods, as he had learned enough of the interesting stranger.

That was just what the youth had hoped to do, and the success of his scheme would have been perfect had the others imitated their wounded companion, but they did not.

Without paying any attention to Sterry they broke into a gallop toward the middle of the river, their course such as to place them either in advance of Fred and Jennie Whitney or to bring all together.

Greatly alarmed for his friends, Monteith did an unnecessary thing by shouting (for the couple could not fail to see their danger), and fired two more barrels of his pistol. Neither shot took effect, nor did the wolves give them any heed, but they and the skaters converged with perilous swiftness.

Forgetful of his own danger, Monteith shouted again:

"Look out! Why don't you change your course?"

Neither replied, but it was absurd for the panic-stricken youth to suppose they did not understand the situation and were shaping their movements accordingly.

Having observed the wolves as soon as Sterry, they never lost sight of them for a second. Every action was watched, and the curious proceeding noted the instant made.

Fred and Jennie continued gliding straight forward, as if they saw them not, and a collision appeared inevitable. At the moment when Monteith's heart stood still, the couple turned almost at right angles to the left—that is, in exactly the opposite direction from the course of the wolves—and in a second they were fifty feet nearer that shore than the brutes. Then followed another quick turn, and they were gliding with arrowy speed straight down stream. They had simply passed around the animals, who, detecting the trick, made their limbs rigid and slid over the ice, with their claws scratching it, until able to check their speed to allow them to turn and resume the pursuit.

Sterry was on the point of uttering a shout of exultation and admiration at the clever manoeuvre, when Jennie cried out; and well might she do so, for fifty yards beyond, and directly in their path, the ice seemed suddenly to have become alive with the frightful creatures, who streamed from the woods on both sides, ravenous, fierce and unrestrainable in their eagerness to share in the expected feast.

Edward S. Ellis

CHAPTER III

THE FLIGHT OVER THE ICE

The same minute that Monteith Sterry saw the new peril which threatened them all he darted out beside the brother and sister, who had slackened their pace at sight of the wolves in front.

"What shall we do?" asked Fred; "we cannot push on; let's go up stream."

"You cannot do that," replied Jennie, "for they are gathering behind us."

A glance in that direction showed that she spoke the truth. It looked as if a few minutes would bring as many there as in advance.

"We shall have to take to the woods," said Fred, "and there's little hope there."

"It won't do," added the sister, who seemed to be thinking faster than either of her companions. "The instant we start for the shore they will be at our heels. Make as if we were going to run in close to the right bank, so as to draw them after us; then turn and dash through them."

The manoeuvre was a repetition of the one she and her brother had executed a few minutes before, and was their only hope.

"I will take the lead with my pistol," said Monteith, "while you keep as close to me as you can."

Every second was beyond value. The wolves were not the creatures to remain idle while a conference was under way. At sight of the three figures near the middle of the course they rent the air with howls, and came trotting toward them with that light, springy movement shown by a gaunt hound, to whom the gait is as easy as a walk.

Monteith Sterry shot forward on his right foot, his revolver, with its two precious charges, tightly gripped in his naked hand.

This was to be called into play only in the last extremity. The killing of a couple of wolves from such a horde could produce no effect upon the rest, unless perhaps to furnish some of them a lunch, for one of the curious traits of the *lupus* species is that they are cannibals, so to speak.

His hope was that the flash and report of the weapon would frighten the animals into opening a path for a moment, through which the skaters could dart into the clear space below.

Having started, Monteith did not glance behind him. Fred and his sister must look out for themselves. He had his hands more than full.

With a swift, sweeping curve he shot toward the bank, the brutes immediately converging to head him off. The slight, familiar scraping on the ice told him that Fred and Jennie were at his heels. He kept on with slackening speed until close to the shore, and it would not do to go any further. An overhanging limb brushed his face.

But his eye was on the wolves further out in the stream. The place was one of the few ones where the course was such that no shadow was along either bank. The moment most of the creatures were drawn well over toward the right shore, Sterry did as his friends did awhile before, skimming abruptly to the left and almost back over his own trail, and then darting around the pack. The line was that of a semicircle, whose extreme rim on the left was several rods beyond the last of the wolves swarming to the right.

"Now!" called Sterry at the moment of turning with all the speed at his command.

Critical as was the moment, he flung one glance behind him. Fred and Jennie were almost nigh enough to touch him with outstretched hand. No need of shouting any commands to them, for they understood what he was doing, or rather trying to do.

Young Sterry, as I have said, had cleared the horde of wolves, making the turn so quickly that they slid a rod or more over the ice before able to check themselves and change their own course.

The stratagem seemed as successful as the other, but it was too soon to congratulate themselves. At the moment when everything promised well, the most enormous wolf he had ever seen bounded from under the trees on the left bank and galloped directly for him.

He was so far in advance that the only way of dodging him was by another sharp turn in his course. To do this, however, would bring him so near the other brutes that they were almost certain to leap upon every one of the party.

"Use your revolver!" called Fred from the rear.

Monteith had already decided that this was an exigency demanding one of the remaining charges, and he partly raised the weapon in front of him.

Meanwhile, the huge wolf had stopped on seeing that the procession was coming in a straight line for him. The youth moderated his speed still more, that he might perfect his aim.

He was in the act of levelling his pistol, when the animal advanced quickly a couple of steps and made a tremendous leap at his throat. The act was unexpected, but at the instant of his leaving the ice Monteith let fly with one chamber at him.

The success was better than he had a right to expect, for the leaden pellet bored its way through the skull of the wolf, who, with a rasping yelp, made a sidelong plunge, as if diving off a bank into the water, and, striking on the side of his head, rolled over on his back, with his legs vaguely kicking at the moon, and as powerless to do harm as a log of wood.

Brief as was the halt, it had given the leading brutes of the main body time to come up. They were fearfully near, when the scent of blood and the sight of their fallen comrade suggested to the foremost that a meal was at their disposal. They flew at the huge fellow and rended him to shreds and fragments in a twinkling.

The only way of escape was still in front, and, with the utmost energy, power, and skill at his command, Monteith

Edward S. Ellis

Sterry darted ahead. His crouching body, the head well in advance, somewhat after the manner of a racing bicyclist on the home-stretch, his compressed lips, his flashing eyes, with every muscle tense, were proof that he knew it had now become a struggle of life and death.

If he allowed one of those wolves to approach nigh enough to leap upon him, he would be borne to the earth like a flash and share the fate of the victim of his pistol. They were near, for he could hear that multitudinous pattering on the ice, when the din of their cries permitted it, and they were running fast.

But, he reasoned, if they were so close to him they must be still closer to the brother and sister, whose peril, therefore, was correspondingly greater. He looked around. He was farther from the horde than he supposed, but Fred and Jennie were not directly behind him, as he had thought.

At the moment an awful thrill shot through him; he caught a glimpse of Fred close in shore and going like the wind. The couple were still preserved from the fangs of the wolves, but only heaven knew how long it would last.

A short distance ahead an opening showed where a creek put in from the woods and hills. Monteith gave it only a glance when he skimmed past at the same furious pace as before. It looked as if there was hope at last, for the brutes first seen were all at the rear. If new danger came, it would be from others that ran out on the ice in front.

"It seems to me that all the wolves in Maine are on this little river," was his thought, "but there may be a few left that will try to get into our path."

A wild cry came from his friends and he glanced toward

them. Not only that, but believing his help was needed, he sheered over to them as quickly as he could.

The course of the river had changed, so that a ribbon of shadow extended along that bank, partially obscuring the form of Fred Whitney, who seemed to cling to it as if therein lay his safety.

The brutes were now so far to the rear that there was little to be feared from them, though they still kept up the pursuit, and while able to follow in a straight line were doing so with more speed than would be expected.

It struck Sterry that his friend was not skating with his utmost skill. He was alarmed.

"What's the matter, Fred?" he called, drawing quickly near him.

"O, Jennie! Jennie! What will become of her?"

Fred Whitney, it was now apparent, was alone.

Forgetful of the savage brutes, Monteith Sterry slackened his pace, and in a scared voice demanded:

"What has become of her? Where is she?"

"She darted into the mouth of that creek."

"Why didn't you follow?"

"I could not; it was done in a flash; she called to me to keep on and said something else which I could not catch."

"But," continued the wondering Monteith, "how could she do

it when she was at your side?"

"She fell a little to the rear and made a lightning turn. I attempted to follow, but it seemed half the pack were in my path, and it was certain death. I was frantic for the moment, and even now do not understand what it all meant."

"What a woeful mistake!" wailed Monteith; "the chances are a thousand to one that she is lost."

"I think," said the brother, half beside himself, "that it may have been a good thing, but—"

A peculiar cry behind them caused Monteith to turn his head. The wolves had gained so fast during the last few minutes that one of them was in the act of springing on Fred Whitney.

"Stoop, quick!" shouted his companion.

Fred bent low in the nick of time, and the gaunt, lank body shot over his head, landing on the ice in front. Before he could gather himself a bullet from the revolver was driven into his vitals and he rolled over and over, snapping and yelping in his death-throes.

The skaters swerved aside enough to avoid him, and the next instant were skimming over the ice at their utmost speed.

It was not a moment too soon, for the halt was well-nigh fatal; but they could travel faster than the animals, and steadily drew away from them until, ere long, they were safe, so far as those creatures were concerned. They continued the pursuit, however, being a number of rods to the rear and in plain sight of the fugitives, who looked back, while speeding forward with undiminished swiftness.

But the couple could not continue their flight, knowing nothing of the missing one. The wolves were between them and her, and Monteith Sterry had fired the last shot in his revolver.

"How far back does that tributary reach?" he asked.

"I never learned, but probably a good way."

"Its breadth is not half of this."

"No; nothing like it."

"What has become of her?"

"Alas! alas! What shall I answer?"

"But, Fred, she is not without hope; she can skate faster than either of us, and I am sure none of them was in front of her on the creek or she would not have made the turn she did."

"If the creek extends for several miles, that is with enough width to give her room, she will outspeed them; but how is she to get back?"

"What need that she should? When they are thrown behind she can take off her skates and continue homeward through the woods, or she may find her way back to the river and rejoin us."

"God grant that you are right; but some of the wolves may appear in front of her, and then—"

"Don't speak of it! We would have heard their cries if any of them had overtaken her."

No situation could be more trying than that of the two youths, who felt that every rod toward home took them that distance farther from the beloved one whose fate was involved in awful uncertainty.

"This won't do," added Monteith, after they had skated some distance farther; "we are now so far from the animals that they cannot trouble us again; we are deserting her in the most cowardly manner."

"But what shall we do? What *can* we do?"

"You know something of this part of the country; let's take off our skates and cut across the creek; she may have taken refuge in the limb of a tree and is awaiting us."

"Isn't some one coming up stream?" asked Fred, peering forward, where the straight stretch was so extensive that the vision permitted them to see unusually far.

"It may be another wolf."

"No; it is a person. Perhaps Quance has been drawn from his home by the racket. He is a great hunter. I hope it is he, for he can give us help in hunting for Jennie—"

Monteith suddenly gripped the arm of his friend.

"It is not a man! It is a woman!"

"Who can it be? Not Jennie, surely—"

"Hurry along! You are no skaters at all!"

It was she! That was her voice, and it was her slight, girlish figure skimming like a swallow toward them.

Within the following minute Fred Whitney clasped his beloved sister in his arms, both shedding tears of joy and gratitude.

Jennie had had a marvellous experience, indeed. Controlled by an intuition or instinct which often surpasses reason, she was led to dart aside into the smaller stream at the critical moment when the fierce wolves were so near that escape seemed impossible. She had fallen slightly to the rear, and a single terrified glance showed her a beast in the act of leaping at her. Her dart to the left was only the effort to elude him for that instant, and she was not aware of the mouth of the creek until she had entered it. Then, seeing that it was altogether too late to rejoin her brother, she had no course left but to continue the flight which, until then, she had not intended.

The words which she called to Fred, that were not understood by him, were to the effect that she would try to rejoin him farther down the stream, with whose many turnings she was more familiar than he.

She ascended the tributary with all the wonderful skill at her command. Not only the brute that was on the point of leaping at her, but three others, turned as soon as they could poise themselves and went after her at their utmost bent.

But her change of direction was a most fortunate action. As in the case of the abrupt darting aside, when on the surface of the larger stream, it placed her considerably in advance of the nearest pursuers. Add to this her power of outspeeding them when the chance was equal, and it will be seen that her only danger was from the front.

The creek was so narrow that if any of the wolves appeared before her she would be lost, for there was not room to manoeuvre as on the larger stream.

But she met none. The first signals had drawn them to the river, and if there were any near, they and she were mutually unaware of it.

As her brother had said, she was more acquainted with this section than he. She knew at what points the river and its tributary curved so as to bring them near each other. Reaching that place, she buried the heels of her skate-runners in the ice, sending the particles about her in a misty shower, and quickly came to a halt. Then, standing motionless, she listened.

In the distance sounded the howling of the animals so repeatedly disappointed of their prey, but none was nigh enough to cause her misgiving.

"I hope no harm has come to Fred or Monteith," she murmured. "Both can skate fast enough to leave the wolves behind; they would have done so at once if they had not been bothered by having me with them. Now they ought to be able to take care of themselves."

She sat down on the bank and removed her skates. The slight layer of snow on the leaves caused no inconvenience, for she was well shod, and the walk was not far. Her fear was that some of the wolves might sneak up unseen. Often she stopped and listened, but when half the distance was passed, without any alarm from that source, she believed nothing was to be feared. A little farther and she reached the main stream, the distance passed being so much less than was necessary for her escorts that she knew that she was in advance of them, even if they had continued their flight without interruption.

Her club skates were securely refastened, and then she listened again.

The cries of the brutes were few and distant and could not cause alarm.

Hark! A familiar sound reached her. She recognized it as made by skates gliding over the ice. Rising to her feet, she remarked, with a smile:

"I think I will give them a surprise." And she did. The meeting was a happy one, and before the stroke of midnight all three were at home, where they found the mother anxiously awaiting their return and greatly relieved to learn that despite their stirring experience no harm had befallen any member of the little party.

CHAPTER IV

THE REPORT OF GUNS

And now comes a change of scene and incident.

Hugh Whitney returned to his Maine home a few weeks after the stirring adventures of his children and Monteith Sterry with the wolves. He was so pleased with the western country that he made his decision to remove thither. He met with no difficulty in selling at a fair price his little property in the Pine-Tree State, and with a portion of the proceeds he bought a ranch near the headwaters of Powder River, to which place he removed, with his family, in the spring of 1890, directly after the incidents related in the preceding chapters.

One of the pleasures of this radical change of residence and occupation was that it was pleasing to his son Fred and his twin sister Jennie, now about nineteen years of age.

Whether the wife shared in the desire to make her home in that new country, or whether she expressed the wish to do so because she saw it would gratify her husband, cannot be said with certainty. There was no doubt, however, about the eagerness with which the brother and sister took part in the removal.

Young, ardent, and of sturdy frame, with all the natural yearning of imaginative youth for adventure, the prospect was an inviting one to them. Their father's glowing accounts of the magnificent scenery, its vast resources and limitless possibilities, caused a yearning on their part probably deeper than his own.

It is rare that such expectations are fully realized in this life. It cannot be said that those of the brother and sister found more than a partial fulfilment, but, though the fateful day came when they regretted the change beyond the power of language to express, yet it was many months before it dawned upon them.

Hugh Whitney's herd of cattle numbered several thousand, and, on the day when we take up the eventful history of the family, they were grazing on the open ranges along the spurs of the Big Horn Mountains.

The two cowmen engaged by Whitney to assist him in the duty of looking after his property were Budd Hankinson and Grizzly Weber. They were veterans in the business, brave and true and tried. Under their tuition, and that of his father, Fred Whitney became a skilful horseman and rancher. He learned to lasso and bring down an obdurate steer, to give valuable help in the round-ups, to assist in branding the registered trademark of his father on the haunches of his animals.

This brand consisted of a cross, with two stars above, one below, the initial letter of his given name on the left, and that of his surname on the right. When this was burned into the flesh of the yearlings, it identified his property, no matter where wandering, and the honest rancher would no more disturb it than he would enter another's home and rob him of his clothing.

The first year was an enjoyable one to Jennie. Her father presented her with an excellent animal, of which she became very fond. A good horsewoman when in Maine, in Wyoming she acquired a skill which compelled the admiration of the cowmen themselves.

"She's struck her callin'," remarked Budd Hankinson one day, while watching her speeding like a courser across the open country.

"What is that?" asked the father, who was proud of his children, and especially of the pretty daughter.

"Why, riding hosses like a streak of lightnin'," was the somewhat indefinite response.

"What particular profession can she fill by dashing over the country in that style?" continued the parent with a smile.

"Why, showing other persons how it is done. I've no doubt, colonel, that she could make good wages in breaking broncos and teaching young women like her how to ride in the right style; I advise you to think about it."

"I will do so," replied the parent, with so much gravity that the cowman never suspected his sincerity, but felt the satisfaction of believing he had given his employer a valuable "pointer."

Another pleasure which followed the removal of the Whitneys to Wyoming was that their friend Monteith Sterry followed them within a few months. He had shown some signs of running down in health while attending the high school in Boston, despite the fact that he was one of the best athletes in the institution; but he readily persuaded his wealthy father that a few months' experience in the bracing northwest would do him more good than anything and everything else in the world.

That he might have some pretext other than the one which could not wholly deceive the Whitneys, he engaged to serve the Live Stock Association, which was beginning to have trouble with the rustlers. Matters were not only going wrong, but were rapidly getting worse in Wyoming, and they were glad to secure the services of such a daring and honest youth, who seemed rather to welcome the fact that he could perform his duties faithfully only at personal risk to himself.

It need not be explained how it came about that young Sterry found it necessary to give a great deal of his attention to that section of Wyoming in which the Whitneys lived. There appeared to be more need of it there than in any of the other neighborhoods where the outlook was really threatening.

The natural consequence was that he became a frequent visitor at the home of his former friend, though he found other acquaintances engaged in the cattle business who were glad to have him take shelter under their roofs. Sometimes he engaged in hunting with them, and several times Fred Whitney and Jennie joined him. There was a spice of peril in these excursions which rendered them fascinating to all three.

The particular day to which we refer was a mild afternoon in May, 1892. Jennie was helping her mother with her household duties in their home, where they had lived since coming from their native State. The building was one of the long, low wooden structures common in that section, to which the fashions of the older civilization have not yet penetrated. It possessed all the comforts they required, though it took some time for the brother and sister to accustom themselves to the odd style of architecture.

Edward S. Ellis

Jennie, as usual, was in high spirits. She had been out for a ride during the forenoon, and was now trying to make up for it by taking the burden of most of the work upon her comely shoulders.

In the middle of one of her snatches of song she abruptly paused with the question:

"Did you hear that, mother?"

"No; to what do you refer?"

"The sound of rifle-firing; something is wrong on the range."

The two paused and listened, looking in each other's pale countenances as they did so.

"It *is* rifle-firing!" said Mrs. Whitney in a scared voice; "what can it mean?"

"Trouble with the rustlers," replied Jennie, hurrying through the open door to the outside that she might hear the better. Her mother followed, and the two stood side by side, listening and peering across the wide stretch of undulating plain in the direction of the mountains, whose wooded crests were outlined against the clear spring sky.

There could be no mistaking the alarming sounds. They were made by rifles, fired sometimes in quick succession, often mingling with each other, and then showing comparatively long intervals between the discharges of the weapons.

"Father said the rustlers were becoming bolder," remarked Jennie, "and there was sure to be trouble with them before long."

"It has come," was the comment of the parent, "and who shall tell the result?"

"It cannot last long, mother."

"A few minutes is a good while at such a time. A score of shots have already been fired, and some of them must have done execution."

"Father, Fred and our two men are unerring shots."

"And so are they," responded the mother, referring to the rustlers, who have made so much trouble for the cattlemen of Wyoming.

Edward S. Ellis

CHAPTER V

LOOKING SOUTHWARD

Mrs. Whitney and her daughter Jennie stood at the door of their ranch listening, with rapidly beating hearts, to the sounds of rifle-firing from the direction of the cattle-range where the beloved husband and son were looking after their property.

Three shots came in quick succession; then, after the interval of a full minute, two more followed, and then all was still.

Mother and daughter maintained their listening attitude a while longer, but nothing more reached their ears.

"It is over," said the parent in an undertone.

Aye, the conflict was over. One party was beaten off, but which? And how many brave men, the finest horsemen and rifle-shots in the world, lay on the green sward, staring, with eyes that saw not, at the blue sky, or were being borne away by their comrades on the backs of their tough ponies?

A brief space and the story would be told.

Jennie Whitney shaded her eyes with her hand and gazed to

the southward for the first sight of returning friends, whose coming could not be long delayed.

The mother was straining her vision in the same direction, watching for that which she longed and yet dreaded to see. But years had compelled her to use glasses, and her eyes were not the equal of those bright orbs of Jennie. She would be the first to detect the approaching horsemen.

A good field-glass was in the house, but neither thought of it; their attention was too deeply absorbed.

"It is time they appeared," remarked Mrs. Whitney, her heart sinking under the dreadful fear of the possible reason why they remained invisible.

Suppose there was none to appear!

But those keen eyes of the maiden have detected something, and she starts and peers more intently than before.

Far to the southward, in the direction of the mountain spurs, and on the very boundary of her vision, a black speck seems to be quivering and flickering, so indistinct, so impalpable, that none but the experienced eye can guess its nature.

But the eye which is studying it is an experienced one. Many a time it has gazed across the rolling prairie, and identified the loved father and brother before another could discover a person at all.

"Some one is coming," she says to her mother.

"Some one!" is the alarmed response; "are there no more?"

"There may be, but this one is in advance."

"But why should he be in advance of the rest?" is the query, born of the fear in the heart of the parent.

"It is not mine to answer for the present; he may be better mounted and is coming for—for—"

"For what?"

"Help."

"Help! What help can we give them?"

"We have a gun in the house, and there is plenty of ammunition."

"That means they have suffered—have been defeated. Look closely, Jennie; do you see no others?"

She has been searching for them from the first. The approaching horseman is now fully defined against the dark-green of the mountains, and the country for half a mile is in clear view.

Over this broad expanse Jennie Whitney's eyes rove, and her heart seems to stand still as she answers:

"He is alone; I see no others."

"Then he brings evil tidings! Our people have been defeated; more than one has fallen."

The approaching horseman was riding furiously. His fleet animal was on a dead run, his neck outstretched, mane and tail streaming as he thundered through the hurricane created by his own tremendous speed.

The man who sat in the saddle was a perfect equestrian, as are all the cowmen and rustlers of the West. He leaned forward, as if he would help his horse to reach his goal at the earliest instant. His broad-brimmed hat fitted so well that it kept its place on his head without any fastening; but his own long, dark locks fluttered over his brawny shoulders, while the trusty Winchester was held in a firm grasp across the saddle in front, where it could be used on the second needed.

Jennie Whitney was studying him closely, for he must be father, brother, or one of the two hired men. She was praying that he was a relative, but it was not so.

The mother could now distinguish the horseman plainly, though not as much so as her daughter.

"I think it is father," she said, speaking her hope rather than her conviction.

"No; it is not he," replied the daughter.

"Then it is Fred."

"No; you are mistaken; it is Budd."

"Alas and alas! why should it be he, and neither my husband nor son?" wailed the parent.

Jennie was right. The man was the veteran cowboy, Budd Hankinson, who had whirled the lasso on the arid plains of Arizona, the Llano Estacado of Texas and among the mountain ranges of Montana; who had fought Apaches in the southwest, Comanches in the south and Sioux in the north, and had undergone hardships, sufferings, wounds and privations before which many a younger man than he had succumbed.

No more skilful and no braver ranchman lived.

Budd had a way of snatching off his hat and swinging it about his head at sight of the ladies. It was his jocular salutation to them, and meant that all was well.

But he did not do so now. He must have seen the anxious mother and daughter almost as soon as they discerned him. Jennie watched for the greeting which did not come.

"Something is amiss," was her conclusion.

The hoofs of the flying horse beat the hard ground with a regular rhythm, and he thundered forward like one who knew he was bringing decisive tidings which would make the hearts of the listeners stand still.

The black eyes of the cowman were seen gleaming under his hat-rim as he looked steadily at the couple, against whom his horse would dash himself the next minute, like a thunderbolt, unless checked.

No fear, however, of anything like that. He rounded to in front of the women, and halted with a suddenness that would have flung a less skilful rider over his head, but which hardly caused Budd Hankinson a jar.

He read the questioning eyes, and before the words could shape themselves on the pallid lips he called out:

"The mischief is to pay!"

"What is it, Budd?" asked Jennie, she and her mother stepping close to his box-stirrup.

"We have had a fight with the rustlers—one of the worst I

ever seed—there was eight of 'em."

"Was anybody—hurt?" faltered the mother.

"Wal, I reckon; three of them rustlers won't rustle again very soon, unless that bus'ness is carried on below, where they've gone; two others have got holes through their bodies about the size of my hat."

"But—but were any of our people injured?" continued the parent, while Jennie tried to still the throbbing of her heart until the answer came.

"Wal, yes," replied Budd, removing his hat and passing his handkerchief across his forehead, as though the matter was of slight account; "I'm sorry to say some of us got it in the neck."

"Who—who—how was it? Don't trifle!"

"Wal, you see Zip Peters rode over from Capt. Whiting's to tell us about the rustlers, and he hadn't much more'n arriv, when along come the others behind him with one of our branded steers. I made them give him up, and then the fight was on. Zip got a piece of lead through the body and the arm, and went out of the saddle without time to say good-by. My hip was grazed twice, but it didn't amount to nothin'; I'm as good as ever. Grizzly lost a piece of his ear, but he bored the rustler through that done it, so that account was squared."

"Then father and Fred were not hurt?" gasped Jennie, clasping her hands and gazing inquiringly into the face of the messenger.

"Wal," he replied, with the same exasperating coolness he had shown after his first exclamation, "I wish I could say that, but it ain't quite so good."

"What—what of my husband?" demanded Mrs. Whitney, stepping so close that she laid her hand on the knee of the sturdy horseman; "tell me quick; and what of Fred, my son?"

"Fred fought like a house afire; he killed one of the rustlers, but his horse was shot and Fred got it through the arm, which ended his power to do much fighting, but he laid down behind his hoss and kept it up like the trump he is."

"Then he isn't badly injured?"

"Bless your heart! of course not; he will be all right in a few days; his arm wants a little nursing, that's all. In the midst of the rumpus who should ride up but Mont Sterry, as he had heard the firing, and the way he sailed in was beautiful to behold. It reminded me of the times down in Arizona when Geronimo made it so lively. He hadn't much chance to show what he could do, for the rustlers found they had bitten off more than they could chaw, and they skyugled after he had dropped one."

The wife and mother drew a sigh of relief, but the daughter was far from satisfied. A dreadful fear in her heart had not yet been quelled.

Her quick perceptions noticed that Budd had said nothing more about her father than to mention the fact that he had been wounded. The mother, in her distress and anxiety, caught at a hope as an assurance which the daughter could not feel.

At the same time Jennie saw that, despite the apparent nonchalance of the messenger and his assumed gayety, he was stirred by some deep emotion.

"He is keeping back something, because he fears to tell it," was her correct conclusion.

CHAPTER VI

COWMEN AND RUSTLERS

Jennie Whitney saw something else, which almost made her heart stop beating.

To the southward, whence Budd Hankinson had ridden, several horsemen were in sight, coming from the direction of the cattle-ranges. They were approaching at a walk, something they would not do unless serious cause existed.

The messenger had been sent ahead to break the news to the sad and anxious hearts.

"Budd," she said, "you have not told us about father."

"Why, yes, my dear," interposed her mother, as if to shut out all evil tidings; "nothing has happened to him."

"Wal, I'm sorry to say that he has been hurt worse than Fred," was the alarming response, accompanied by a deep sigh.

"How bad? How much worse? Tell us, tell us," insisted the wife.

"Thar's no use of denyin' that he got it bad; fact is he couldn't have been hit harder."

The distressed fellow was so worked up that he turned his head and looked over his shoulder, as if to avoid those yearning eyes fixed upon him. That aimless glance revealed the approaching horsemen and nerved him with new courage.

"Now, Mrs. Whitney and Jennie, you must be brave. Bear it as he would bear the news about you and Fred if he was— alive!"

A shriek accompanied the words of the cowman, and Jennie caught her mother in time to save her from falling. Her own heart was breaking, but she did her utmost, poor thing, to cheer the one to whom the sunlight of happiness could never come again.

"There, mother, try to bear it. We have Fred left to us, and I am with you. God will not desert us."

Hugh Whitney had never spoken after that first interchange of volleys with the rustlers. He died bravely at the post of duty and was tenderly borne homeward, where he was given a decent burial, his grave bedewed not only by the tears of the stricken widow and children, but by those of the stern, hardy cowmen to whom he had been an employer as kind and indulgent as he was brave.

A few paragraphs are necessary to explain the incidents that follow.

Wherever cattlemen have organized outfits and located ranches cattle-thieves have followed, and fierce fighting has resulted. These men are known as "rustlers." The late troubles caused cattle and horse-thieves to unite against the legitimate owners, and the name now includes both classes of evil-doers. The troubles in Wyoming were the results of the efforts of the Wyoming State Live Stock Association to put a check upon rustlers who are tempted to steal by the vast profits afforded.

At the time the Association was formed the rustlers were few in number, and confined their acts to branding the mavericks or unbranded yearlings with their own brands. They did not act in concert, and since the laws of the State require every brand to be registered, in order to establish ownership, the rustlers had as much right to their own brands as the legitimate cowmen. As long as the mavericks were not openly branded there was no means of stopping them.

It happens quite often that the round-up fails to gather in all the cattle. The mavericks are allowed to go to the outfit with whose cattle they have run, and that outfit puts its own brand on them.

The rustlers grew more daring as their numbers increased, and, instead of confining their operations to the mavericks, began altering brands. Not only that, but they were often bold enough to leave the old brand and burn a new one and forge a bill of sale.

The rustlers were generally the owners of small ranches, or cowboys who had a few head of cattle on the range or running with some rancher's stock. The Association made a rule that no cow outfit should employ a cowman that had been guilty of branding a maverick, or of helping the rustlers, or of working with or for them. A blacklist was kept of such cowmen, with the result that a good many were unable to get employment from the Association outfits and were compelled to become rustlers themselves.

The association of rustlers became desperate because of the serious check given them by the Live Stock Association, which placed its inspectors at all the cattle-markets, Omaha, Chicago, St. Louis, Kansas City and St. Paul. Every shipment of cattle was closely inspected, and if it came from a rustler he was obliged to prove his title to each steer, or they were confiscated and the proceeds sent to the owner of the brand. Sometimes a legal proof of ownership would not be accepted, for the owners were determined to stamp out the rustling business.

Deprived by this means of a market for their hoof cattle, the rustlers were compelled to butcher their cattle or drive to Montana. The latter recourse was not only difficult and dangerous, but there was no certainty of a market when accomplished, as the Live Stock Association kept a vigilant watch on all Wyoming cattle.

The other scheme was unsatisfactory, but it was all that was left to the rustlers. They employed a number of butchers at Buffalo to do their killing for them, but even then they were not sure of always getting their meat marketed.

In the summer of 1891 the rustlers ran waggons openly on all the three great round-ups, and worked the round-up just as if they were a regular Association outfit. They also gathered in all the mavericks, and no one dared interfere.

It should be added that no more dangerous set of men can be found anywhere than the Wyoming rustlers. No living being excels them in horsemanship. The bucking pony is as a child in their hands. There is not one among them who cannot rope, throw, tie and brand a steer single-handed. They include the best riders and the best shots in the cattle business. They do not know what fear is, and in the year named became strong enough to elect one of their own number sheriff.

CHAPTER VII

THE WARNING

The full moon was shining on the second night succeeding the conflict which Budd Hankinson described between the rustlers and the cowmen of Whitney's ranch. The man that had fallen was laid away in a grave back of the house, and mother, son and daughter mourned him with a sorrow that was soothed by the consciousness that he had been a good husband and father in every sense of the word.

On this night, before the hour was late, three persons were seated in the balmy air on the outside of the dwelling, talking together in low tones.

They were Fred Whitney, whose bandaged arm rested in a sling, Monteith Sterry, and Jennie Whitney. The memory of the recent affliction suffered in the death of the father naturally subdued the voices and tinged the words with a seriousness that would not have been felt at other times.

Young Sterry, as already stated, had accepted an engagement with the Live Stock Association, which required him to investigate the operations of the rustlers over a large portion of Wyoming and Montana, and to report at regular intervals to his superior officers.

This was perilous business, but Sterry set about the work with a vigour, directness and intelligence that were felt over an extent of territory numbering hundreds of square miles, and made him a marked man by the rustlers, who are always quick to identify their friends and enemies. It seemed to make little difference, however, to him, who loved the excitement. He was a capital pistol and rifle-shot, a fine horseman, and as devoid of fear as the men against whom he directed his movements.

Unconsciously Monteith Sterry brought a grievous peril upon his friends, who held him in so high regard. Hated intensely by the rustlers, they were not long in learning that he spent a great deal of his time at the Whitneys. They came to be regarded, therefore, as aiders and abettors of his. This enmity was emphasized by the attack of which an account has been given.

"I think, Fred," said his sister, oppressed by the shadow that had fallen across the threshold, "we ought to sell out and leave this country."

"Why?" he gently asked.

"Because not only of what happened yesterday, but of the certainty that such attacks will be repeated."

"What reason have you to fear their repetition?" asked Monteith.

"Matters are growing worse between the cowmen and the rustlers; I have heard our men talk, and you have said so yourself."

"I cannot deny it," replied their visitor, thoughtfully smoking his cigar. He would have been pleased had her brother, now the head of the little household, decided to make his home once more in the East, for then he would take up the study of his profession of law and be placed where he could often meet them.

"It would be cowardly to sell out and abandon the country through fear of those men," said the brother, to whom the proposition was not pleasant.

"But suppose you should be their next victim?" suggested Jennie, with a shudder.

"I don't think I shall be a victim," he quietly responded; "this wound won't bother me long, and with Budd and Grizzly to help, we can laugh at all the rustlers in the country."

"It is hardly a matter of courage," ventured Sterry, "for no one knowing you or your sister would question your bravery, but it is rather the peace of mind of your mother and her. It will be a long time, if ever, before your parent recovers from the shock of yesterday. No matter how confident and plucky you may be, Fred, you know it is no guarantee against a bullet from one of those scamps at five hundred or a thousand yards. I shudder to think of what might happen."

Fred turned and looked full in the handsome face of the fellow beside him.

"It strikes me that you are showing little faith in your own words. Why do you remain where you are a marked man when there is no need of it, and where your personal danger is certainly as great as mine?"

This *argumentum ad hominem* was so unexpected that Sterry was embarrassed for the moment, but found voice to reply:

"I have no mother and sister dependent on me, as you have."

"But you have brothers, sisters, father and mother, and therefore the more to mourn if you should fall. The fact is, Mont, I feel that it is a duty you owe to them to give up the dangerous calling you have adopted. You not only do not need it, but are squandering time that ought to be given to the study of your profession, and you have become so feared and hated by the rustlers that they will go to any length to 'remove' you."

"The more cause, therefore, why I should stay," responded the other.

"A poor argument—"

The discussion was interrupted by the sound of a horse's hoofs. Some one was riding toward them on a gallop, and speedily loomed to view in the bright moonlight. The three instinctively ceased speaking and gazed curiously at the horseman, who reined up in front of where they were sitting.

Hospitality is limitless in the West, and, before the stranger had halted, Fred Whitney rose from his chair and walked forward to welcome him.

The man was in the costume of a cowboy, with rifle, revolver and all the paraphernalia of the craft.

"Is your name Whitney?" asked the horseman, speaking first.

"It is; what can I do for you?"

"Do you know Mont Sterry?"

"He is a particular friend of mine," replied Whitney,

Edward S. Ellis

refraining from adding that he was the young man sitting a few paces away with his sister and hearing every word said.

"Well, there's a letter for him; if I knew where to find him I would deliver it myself. Will you hand it to him the next time you meet him?"

As he spoke he leaned forward from his saddle and handed a sealed envelope to Fred Whitney, who remarked, as he accepted it:

"I will do as you wish; I expect to see him soon; won't you dismount and stay over night with us?"

"No; I have business elsewhere," was the curt answer, as the fellow wheeled and spurred off on a gallop.

Budd Hankinson and Grizzly Weber, the two hired men, were absent, looking after the cattle, for the rustler is a night hawk who often gets in the best part of his work between the set and rise of sun.

Mrs. Whitney was sitting in the gloom, alone in her sorrow. Jennie wished to stay with her, but the mother gently refused, saying she preferred to have none with her. No light was burning in the building, and that night the weather was unusually mild.

Mont Sterry accepted the paper from the hand of his friend and remarked, with a smile:

"I suspect what it is. When the rustlers don't like a man they have a frank way of telling him so, supplemented by a little good advice, I fancy I have been honoured in a similar way."

He deliberately tore open the envelope, while Jennie and her brother looked curiously at him. The moonlight, although strong, was not sufficiently so to show the words, which were written in lead-pencil. Fred Whitney, therefore, struck a match and held it in front of the paper, while the recipient read in a low voice, loud enough, however, to be heard in the impressive hush:

"MONT STERRY: If you stay in the Powder River country twenty-four hours longer you are a dead man. Over fifty of us rustlers have sworn to shoot you on sight, whether it is at Fort McKinley, Buffalo, or on the streets of Cheyenne. I have persuaded the majority to hold off for the time named, but not one of them will do so an hour longer, nor will I ask them to do so. We are bound to make an honest living, and it is weak for me to give you this warning, but I do it, repeating that if you are within reach twenty-four hours from the night on which this is handed to Whitney I will join them in hunting you down, wherever you may be.

"LARCH CADMUS."

CHAPTER VIII

GOOD-BYE

Monteith Sterry read the "warning" through in a voice without the slightest tremor. Then he quietly smoked his cigar and looked off in the moonlight, as though thinking of something of a different nature.

It was natural that Jennie Whitney should be more impressed by the occurrence, with the memory of the recent tragedy crushing her to the earth. She exclaimed:

"Larch Cadmus! Why, Fred, he has visited our house several times; he was here last week."

"Yes," replied her brother; "he has often sat at our table; and, by the way, he is a great admirer of yours."

"Nonsense!" was the response; "why do you say that?"

"It may be nonsense, but it is true, nevertheless. Your mother noticed it; and, that there might be no mistake, Larch had the impudence to tell me so himself."

"I never liked him; he is a bad man," said Jennie, much to the relief of Sterry, who felt a little uncomfortable. "I did not know he belonged to the rustlers."

"He was a cowboy until last fall. He had a quarrel with Col. Ringgold and went off with the others, and has been on the blacklist ever since."

"Why didn't he bring the message himself," continued the sister, "instead of sending it?"

"He did," was the significant reply of the brother.

"What! That surely was not he?"

"It was. I knew his voice the moment he spoke; those whiskers were false; he didn't want to be recognized, and I thought it as well to humor his fancy, but I could not be mistaken."

"Now that I recall it, his voice *did* resemble Cadmus'," said the sister, more thoughtfully.

"Of course, and I can tell you something more; he was among the rustlers with whom we had the fight yesterday. He did his best to kill me, and came pretty near succeeding. It wasn't he, however, who put the bullet through my arm, for I dropped that fellow."

"You frighten me!" was all that Jennie Whitney could say.

Sterry still smoked in silence. He was thinking hard, but it was his turn to be startled by the next remark.

"Larch Cadmus hates you, Mont, not so much because you are the enemy of all rustlers, but more because he believes my sister holds you in higher esteem than she does him."

Edward S. Ellis

Sterry was clever enough to parry this compliment with considerable skill.

"For the same reason he is jealous of every gentleman whom Miss Whitney has ever met, for it would be a sorry tribute to any man's worth if he did not stand higher in her regard than Larch Cadmus."

"Well spoken!" said the young lady, relieved from what threatened to become an embarrassing situation for her.

Had her brother chosen he might have expressed what was in his mind, but he had the good taste to refrain. None knew better than he the deep, tender affection existing between his friend and his sister, though it had not yet reached the point of avowal and confession.

"Well, Mont, what are you going to do about it?" asked Whitney.

By way of reply, the latter twisted the "warning" into the form of a lamplighter. Then he applied a match to one corner, and held the paper until it had burned to the last fragment.

"That's my opinion of Mr. Larch Cadmus and his gang, and I shall pay the same attention to them."

"You are not wise," ventured Jennie, who, with the awful memory of the preceding day upon her, could not but shudder at the peril to her friend, who had never been quite so near to her as during the last few hours, when he showed so much tender sympathy for her and her mother and brother in the depth of their desolation and woe.

"I thank you," he said, with the same manly frankness he had always shown; "I have no desire to appear as a boaster or to make light of danger, but one of the truest adages is that it is not the barking dog that does the biting."

"Don't make the mistake of supposing it is not so in this case," said Whitney, "and none should know it better than you."

"I do not underestimate the courage of those fellows; they will shrink at nothing, but there is no more excuse for my running away upon receiving such a warning than there would be for all the inhabitants of Wyoming to leave the State at such a command."

"The case is not parallel," was the comment of Fred Whitney.

"Bear in mind that if I stay, as I intend to do, I do not mean to sit down and wait for those rustlers to pick me off. I count on having something to say and do in the matter; but, friends, I must bid you good-night."

"What do you mean?" asked the astonished Fred Whitney.

"I must leave," replied Sterry, rising to his feet; "I have already staid too long."

CHAPTER IX

A SUMMONS AND A REPLY

Brother and sister were astounded. The hour was late, and they had been urging their guest to remain several days with them. He had not consented, nor had he refused, from which they were confident he would stay.

And now he announced his intention of departing at once, riding out into the night—whither?

They protested, but he replied so earnestly that an urgent necessity existed that they refrained. He gave no hint of the reason for his strange action, and they could not ask it. His fleet mare, which had been allowed to graze on the succulent grass at the rear of the building with the other horses, was brought forward and saddled and bridled, and he quickly vaulted upon her back.

"Remember me to your mother; it is not worth while to disturb her; I hope soon to be with you again."

He leaned over and pressed the hand of Fred Whitney, and then, raising his hat with his left hand, extended the right to Jennie.

Fred made an excuse to move away a few paces, for he understood the situation.

"Good-by," Sterry said in a voice just low enough to reach the dear one, as he pressed the delicate hand which rested so trustingly in his own.

"Good-by," she answered. "I am sorry you are going."

"So am I, but it is better that I should leave. As I said, I trust soon to see you again. Do you know why I hope Fred will decide to return to the East with you and your mother?"

"I suppose because we shall all be safer there;" and then she added, forgetting her sorrow for the moment, "that is if we do not go skating to Wolf Glen."

"It is not necessary to remove as far as Maine, but father insists that I am wasting time here, when I ought to be home studying my profession."

"And he is right, Monteith."

"But," he replied in a low voice, "before I go back I want to make sure that you will do the same. There, good-by again."

He replaced his hat, wheeled and dashed across the prairie without another word.

Jennie stood gazing in the direction taken by him for some time after he had disappeared in the gloom of the night. Then she turned to speak to her brother, but he had passed within the house. She resumed her seat, knowing he would soon return.

Fifteen minutes and more went by and she was still alone.

Sh! Was she mistaken, or was that the faint sound of a horse's hoofs in the distance?

She turned her head and listened. The murmur of voices, as her brother and mother talked in low tones, did not disturb her, and the almost inaudible lowing of the cattle on the distant ranges was but a part of silence itself.

Hardly a breath of air was stirring, but all knew the eccentric way in which sound is sometimes carried by it. Suddenly the reports of rifle-firing were heard, faint but distinct, and lasting several minutes. Then other and different noises reached her, still faint but clear.

Her power of hearing, like her vision, was exceptionally strong. It was that which enabled her to tell that the last sounds were not made by a single animal, but by several going at a high rate of speed. These, with the reports of rifles, made her certain that the rustlers had attacked Sterry.

Meanwhile the young man found matters exceedingly lively.

The reception of the "warning" through the hands of Fred Whitney was proof that his enemies knew he was frequently at his house. Their messenger had gone thither to deliver it. Young Whitney had slain one of their number, and though the law-breakers themselves had suffered the most, they felt bitter resentment toward the family.

If Sterry remained with them they would have trouble. He was satisfied that Larch Cadmus recognized him, as he sat in front of the rancher's house, and would not forget to tell it to his comrades, who would speedily make the place a visit. He believed they were likely to do it before the rise of the morrow's sun.

If the Whitneys were attacked, his presence would add to the defensive strength, but such an attack would not be made if he was not there. Desperate and defiant as the rustlers had been, it would be an injustice to represent them as capable of such wantonness.

He felt, therefore, that it was his duty to leave the ranch without delay, thus removing an element of grave danger. It would have been hardly wise to make this explanation to them, though he believed Fred suspected it.

Turning his back, therefore, upon the dearest spot in all the West to him, he set his mare Queenie on an easy, swift gallop, heading southward toward the ranges where the cattle of the Whitneys were grazing.

Sterry, in one sense, was without a home as long as he remained in Wyoming or Montana, while in another sense he was the owner of numberless dwelling-places or "head-quarters." He may be likened to a commercial traveller in a vast and sparsely-settled region, where he is well known and welcomed by the inhabitants.

The ranchmen who knew him—and there were few who did not—were his friends, for he was working in their interests. At whichever cabin he drew rein he was certain of a hospitable reception.

With no clearly defined idea of where he would spend the remaining hours of the night, he turned the nose of Queenie toward the ranges, among the mountain spurs.

Grizzly Weber and Budd Hankinson would stay near the cattle for an indefinite time, and he was debating whether to join them or to ride on to the ranch of Dick Hawkridge, a number of miles to the northeast, when his meditations were broken in upon in the most startling manner.

During those perilous times, the lonely horseman, in a dangerous region, relies much on his intelligent steed for warning. While Monteith Sterry could do a great deal of thinking in the saddle, he was too alert to drop into a brown study that would divert his thoughts from his surroundings.

He was no more than a mile from the Whitney ranch when his mare pricked up her ears, gave an almost inaudible whinny, and slightly slackened her pace.

That meant that she scented danger, and her rider was on the *qui vive*.

He tightened the rein and drew her to a full stop. She turned her head to the right and looked steadily in that direction, with her pretty ears thrown forward. This meant that whatever impended was coming from that point of the compass.

But the keen eyes of Mont Sterry could not penetrate the moonlight sufficiently far to detect anything. He was out of the saddle in a twinkling, and tried a trick learned from the old hunters. He pressed one ear against the ground, which, as all know, is a much better conductor of sound than the air.

This told the story he anticipated. The faint but distinct clamping of horses' hoofs was heard. The number indefinite, but, somewhat to his surprise, none of them was running or loping; all were moving on a walk.

The noise was so clear that when he rose to his feet and looked off to the right he expected to see the animals and their riders, and he was not disappointed.

On the outer margin of the field of vision the outlines of several horsemen assumed shape. They were approaching, and one of their steeds emitted a whinny, as a salutation to the motionless Queenie, who had shifted her pose so as to face that point of the compass.

"Sh!" whispered Sterry to her.

But there was no call for the warning; she was too well trained to betray her master, and remained mute.

But it was inevitable that if the young man could discern the figures of the approaching horsemen, they must also see him. He leaped into the saddle and turned away.

He knew instinctively they were rustlers, and he was almost equally certain they were hunting for him. There were at least three; and, well aware of their character, he was only prudent in shying off, with the intention of avoiding them altogether.

But they were not the men to be bluffed in that fashion. They were "out" for the inspector, and did not intend that such an opportunity should slip by unchallenged.

"Hello, pard!" called one of the trio, "where from and where going?"

This was a pointed demand, to which Mont Sterry made an equally pointed response.

"That is my own business; I will attend to it, and you may attend to yours."

All this time he was keeping watch of their movements. Their horses were still walking, but they were now coming straight toward him. At a touch of the rein Queenie headed directly away, and her gait was about the same. She acted as though she shared the thoughts of her master, who shrank from sending her off on a flying run, as would have been more prudent for him to do.

A brave man dislikes to flee, even when his better judgment tells him it is the only wise thing to do.

The night was so still that Sterry plainly heard the words of the men when talking to each other in an ordinary conversational tone.

"I believe that's him," said one of them, eagerly.

"It sounded like his voice, but he wouldn't leave the Whitneys at this time of night when she's there."

"He's too free with his tongue, anyway; we'll make him show up."

"Say, you! hold on a minute. Do you know anything about Mont Sterry? We're looking for him."

"I am Mont Sterry," was the defiant response. "What do you propose to do about it?"

CHAPTER X

A HOT PURSUIT

It may be said Mont Sterry answered his own question at the moment of asking it, for, bringing his Winchester to his shoulder, he let fly at the rustlers, and then with a word and touch of the spur sent Queenie bounding away with arrowy swiftness.

Unquestionably it was a daring act on his part, but there was wisdom in it. He knew those men were seeking his life, and would shoot him, as they had threatened to do, on sight. When they met, it would be a question simply as to which got the drop on the other.

They were preparing to make a rush at him, and while he had no fear of a contest of speed between Queenie and any animal that "wore horse-hair," they were altogether too near at the beginning of the contest, and the chance of using their rifles was too much against him.

The crack of the Winchester accompanying his sharp reply, with the whistle of the bullet about their heads, gave them a momentary shock, which delayed the pursuit for a few precious seconds.

Edward S. Ellis

This was the object of the fugitive, for, while that brief interval was thrown away by them, he improved it to the utmost. At such crises a few rods count immensely, and they were made to count on the side of Mont Sterry.

They were insufficient, however, to take him beyond peril. Men like those horsemen are quick to recover from a surprise, and it would have seemed that Sterry was hardly started in his flight when they were speeding after him. He heard their maledictions and knew that the struggle for life was on.

Comparatively brief as had been the time spent in the West by Sterry, he had not neglected his education along the lines indispensable to those following his manner of living. At the moment of giving Queenie rein he flung himself forward on her neck, hugging it close and uttering an involuntary prayer that the bullets might pass harmlessly by him and his horse.

There were enough of the missiles to kill several men, but the chance for aiming was so poor that even such fine marksmen as the rustlers had little chance. The mare was only dimly discernible, and she, like their own horses, was going at full speed.

Had the sun been shining the result must have been widely different.

The encounter with these men was so unexpected and the several changes of direction by Queenie so sudden and unavoidable that Sterry was not given a chance to take his bearings. The one object was to get as far from them as possible in the quickest time in which it could be done.

When that distance became a safe one it would be soon enough to give attention to the points of the compass.

Nobly did Queenie do her duty. She had carried her master out of many a peril, and she could be counted on to do it as long as the ability remained with her. Sterry's anxiety was really more on her account than on his own. He knew there was little danger of himself being struck by the bullets of the rustlers, who, as I have shown, had no possible chance of taking any sort of aim, but she was a conspicuous target, which it would seem they ought to hit with little difficulty.

Often must a person in the situation of Sterry leave everything to his horse. He did not seek to guide Queenie, but sat, or rather lay, in the saddle and on her neck, as she skimmed like a swallow over the undulating prairie.

Strange imaginings were in the brain of the young man during those few minutes. He listened to each shot of the Winchesters, and then, instead of feeling any apprehension for himself, waited for the dreaded evidence that his horse had been struck.

The skilful railway engineer, sitting in his cab, with his hand on the throttle, can discover, on the instant, the slightest disarrangement in the mass of intricate mechanism over which he holds control. His highly trained senses enable him to feel it like a flash. So it was that Mont Sterry would have detected any injury to his horse as quickly as she herself. No matter if but the abrasion of the skin, the puncture of the flesh, or the nipping of an ear, she would betray it involuntarily.

If she were wounded and should fall, the situation of her rider would be well-nigh hopeless. He could only throw himself behind her body and have it out with his enemies. Such a defence has been successfully made many a time by white men against Indians; but Sterry would not be fighting Crows nor Sioux, but those of his own race and blood, as brave and skilful as he.

"Thank God!" he murmured, after each shot, as the splendid play of the machinery under him continued without a break or tremor; "she was not hit that time. She is running at her best."

Once his heart stood still, for she seemed to quiver through her body, as if involuntarily shrinking from the prick of a sword.

In his alarm, Sterry rose to an upright posture in the saddle, and leaning to the right and left, and looking forward and behind him, searched for the wound. He hardly expected to see it, for it would have been beyond his sight in any one of a dozen different portions of the body.

But if in one of the limbs, it would quickly show in the gait of the animal.

"No," he murmured, "there is no change of pace; it could not have been much, and it may be she was not hit at all."

The rustlers fired two shots at this moment, when the horseman was more of a target than his animal, but he gave no heed to that; it was she for whom he felt concern.

A glance backward brought a thrill of hope. The distance between him and his pursuers had perceptibly increased. Queenie was showing her heels to those who dared dispute with her the supremacy of fleetness. She would soon leave them out of sight, unless it should prove she was disabled by some of the shots.

All would have gone well but for the appearance of a new danger of which he did not dream.

Suddenly Queenie emitted her faint, familiar whinny, and swerved to the left. She had scented a new peril.

In the gloom almost directly ahead loomed the figures of other horsemen bearing down upon the fugitive. They might be friends, and they might be enemies, but it would not do to take chances. Without an instant's hesitation Sterry wheeled to the left and spoke to his horse:

"Now, Queenie, do your best."

The mare responded with the same gameness she always showed; but the situation had suddenly become so grave that Monteith Sterry assuredly would have been overwhelmed and cut off but for one of the most extraordinary occurrences that ever came to any person in the extremity of danger.

CHAPTER XI

A STRANGE DIVERSION

It was the wonderful sagacity of the little mare which intervened at this crisis in the fate of her rider.

She was no more than fairly stretched away on a dead run from the new peril when she shot into an arroya or depression in the prairie. Such a depression suggests the dry bed of a stream through which the water may not have flowed for years. It is sometimes a few feet only in width, and again it may be a number of rods. The rich, alluvial soil often causes a luxuriant growth of grass, cottonwood or bush, which affords the best of grazing and refuge for any one when hard pressed by the enemy.

The arroya into which Queenie plunged had gently sloping sides, and was perhaps fifty feet wide. The bottom was covered not only with grass, but with the thin undergrowth to which allusion has been made, and which was so frail in character that it offered no impediment to the passage of a running horse.

Sterry's expectation was that his mare would shoot across the depression and up the other bank with the least possible delay; but of her own accord, and without suggestion from him, she turned abruptly to the left and dropped to a walk.

He was astounded, and was on the point of speaking impatiently to her as he jerked the bridle-rein, when the occurrence already referred to took place, and made the action of the animal seem like an inspiration or instinct approaching the height of reason.

At the moment she made the sharp turn to the left, another horseman galloped up the opposite slope and off upon the prairie. By an amazing coincidence it happened that he was in the arroya, and in the act of crossing in the same direction with the fugitive, when the furious plunge of the mare sent his own bounding up the farther bank.

Sterry caught the situation like a flash. Before Queenie had gone more than a half-dozen rods he brought her to a stand-still. They resembled an equestrian statue, so motionless were they for a full minute.

The converging parties of pursuers could plainly see the second horseman speeding away from the other side, and inevitably concluded that he was the inspector whom they wanted. They were after him hot-footed on the instant.

This man was Ira Inman, a well-known rustler, and the intimate friend of Larch Cadmus. When he saw himself pursued by a half-dozen of his friends he reined up, and calmly but wonderingly awaited their arrival, which took place within the next few seconds.

"Up with your hands! Quick about it, too! You're the man we want!"

"Wal," replied the leader, surveying them with a grin, and paying no heed to their fierce commands, "now that you've got me, what are you going to do with me?"

If there ever were a set of dumbfounded men, they were the rustlers who closed about the leader and recognized him in the moonlight. The remarks that followed his identification were as ludicrous as they were vigourous.

The majority believed he had played a trick on them in pretending to be Mont Sterry, whom all were so anxious to bring down; but there were one or two who were not satisfied. They knew the voice of the inspector, which in no way resembled the gruff tones of Inman. Then, their leader was not given to practical jokes.

"What set you to hunting me so hard?" he asked, after the first flurry was over.

"We're looking for Mont Sterry."

"Wal, what made you take me for him? Do I look like him in the moonlight?"

"But you said you were, and fired at us," explained one.

"Fired at you? Said I was that chap? What in the mischief are you driving at?"

One, who suspected the truth, now interposed.

"We did meet Sterry and hailed him; you must have heard our guns; he dashed into the arroya; we saw you gallop out on t'other side, and took you for him."

"Ah, I understand it all now," replied Inman; "I had ridden down there on my way back from a little scout, when a horseman dashed into the slope behind me like a thunderbolt.

My horse was so scared that he went up the other side on the jump, and before I could turn around to find out what it all meant, you lunkheads came down on me with the request to oblige you by throwing up my hands, which I will see you hanged before I'll do."

"But where is he? What has become of him?" asked several, looking around, as thought they expected to see the young man ride forward and surrender himself.

"Wal, calling to mind the kind of horse he rides, I should say he is about a half-mile off by this time, laughing to find out how cleverly he has fooled you chaps."

"It looks as if you was in the same boat, Inman," retorted one of the chagrined party.

"I wasn't chasing Sterry."

"He seemed to be chasing you, for you came out of the arroya ahead of him."

"If he was chasing me," replied the leader, who felt that the laugh was on his companions, "he would have followed me out; but I don't see anything of him;" and he, too, stared around, as though not sure the man would not do the improbable thing named.

"It was a blamed cute trick, any way you look at it," remarked one of the party. "It was queer that you should have been there, Inman, just at the minute needed. But for that, we would have had him, sure."

"Wal, you can make up your mind that we have him as good as catched already. He can't get out of the country without some of the boys running against him, and the first rustler

Edward S. Ellis

that catches sight of Mr. Sterry will drop him in his tracks."

"If he gets the chance to do it," was the wise comment of another. "That fellow is quick on the shoot and isn't afraid of any of us."

"He ain't the first one that's made that mistake, only to find himself rounded up at last. Larch Cadmus' idea of 24 hours' notice don't go down with this crowd, eh?"

And the crowd unanimously responded in the negative.

CHAPTER XII

THE BACK TRAIL

Mont Sterry had wisdom enough to turn to the fullest account the remarkable advantage gained through the sagacity of his mare.

His pursuers, in their haste to head him off, had dashed across the arroya at a point only a short distance above where he entered and their leader emerged from it. They were sure to discover the truth in a short time.

Waiting, therefore, only until they had passed beyond, he rode his horse a few rods along the depression, and then left it on the same side by which he had ridden into it.

Unconsciously he fell into an error of which he was not dreaming. In the short distance passed, the arroya made a sweeping curve, and he had repeatedly changed his own course since leaving the Whitney ranch. Thus it was almost inevitable that he should get the points of the compass mixed, and that he should follow a route widely different from the one intended.

Had he paused long enough to note the position of the full moon in the heavens, or the towering Big Horn Mountains,

Edward S. Ellis

he would have gained an approximate idea of where he was; but, despite his experience in the West, he galloped forward at an easy canter, with never a suspicion of the blunder he was making.

He was on the alert for rustlers, and kept glancing to the right and left, and to the front and rear. As has been shown, he had little fear of being overtaken in a chase where he was given an equal chance with his pursuers, but his narrow escape rendered him more apprehensive than usual.

"I thought of staying with Weber and Hankinson to-night," he mused, "but I think it hardly prudent. The rustlers may pay them a visit, and my presence will only make matters worse; and yet those fellows don't want to start up a band of regulators who will shoot them down without mercy, and that's just what will take place if they carry their outrages too far."

"My death won't bring the regulators into existence," he grimly reflected, "for one man, more or less, doesn't count; but there is much bitter feeling in the country."

Once he thought he caught the sounds of horses' feet on the prairie, and checked his mare to listen, but she gave no evidence of suspicion—a thing she was sure to do, if the cause existed.

Sterry was so well satisfied by this fact that he did not dismount to test the matter as before. He rode on, however, and held her down to a walk.

His eventless course had continued some minutes before a thought came to him of the direction he was following, with the possibility that he was wrong.

"I wonder if we are on the right track, Queenie?" he said, addressing his animal, as was his custom when they were alone. "It would be strange if we didn't drift away from our bearings. Hello! that can't be Dick Hawkridge's ranch; we haven't gone far enough for that; but what the mischief can it be, unless a fire that some one has started in the open?"

The starlike twinkle of a point of light suddenly shone out directly in advance. It puzzled him by appearing only for a moment, when it vanished as quickly as it entered his field of vision.

This fact suggested that it was within some dwelling and had been extinguished, or was shut from sight by being moved past a window or open door to another point in the interior.

"We are so near, Queenie, we may as well go farther," he added, not unmindful of his danger from those who were making such a hot search for him. He kept his horse on a walk, maintaining a keen watch between the dainty ears that were already pricked up as if she knew something was likely to happen quite soon.

Advancing in this deliberate fashion, the outline of one of those long, low wooden structures so common in the West was gradually defied in the moonlight, and he knew he was approaching the home of some ranchman.

But whose? was the question that perplexed him. He recalled that some of his travelling had been done at a high rate of speed, but the distance between the Whitney and Hawkridge ranches was fully a dozen miles, and he was sure that that space had not been covered by him since bidding his friends good-by earlier in the evening, especially as he had not followed a direct course.

Edward S. Ellis

"Can it be?" he exclaimed, with a sudden suspicion. "Yes, by gracious! What a blunder!"

The exclamation was caused by the sight of a young man, with one arm in a sling, who came forward to welcome him.

He had returned to the Whitney home, which he supposed was miles away, and this was his old friend Fred, who came smilingly forward and said, as he recognized him:

"I am glad, indeed, to see you, Mont; we heard the sound of the firing and feared that something had happened to you."

"Nothing at all, thank you, and nothing to Queenie—but that reminds me," he added, slipping out of the saddle; "she acted once as though she had been hit, though it wasn't bad enough to show itself in her gait."

The two made a hasty examination but discovered nothing; proof that, as her owner said, the wound, if any, was too slight to trouble her.

"Fred, what do you think of my coming back to you in this fashion?" abruptly asked Sterry, with a laugh, looking around in his friend's face.

"The most sensible thing you could have done; it redeems your foolishness in leaving us as you did."

"But my return was involuntary."

"How was that?"

"I thought I was miles distant, and had no idea of my location until I caught the outlines of your house; I assure you I contemplated no such performance as this."

"Well, you're here, so what's the use of talking unless you mean to mount your mare and try it again."

"Hardly that; I have too much mercy on her."

The couple walked past the dwelling to the rude but roomy shelter at the rear where the horses were sometimes placed when not in use, or when the severity of the weather made the protection necessary. There the saddle, bridle and trappings were removed from the mare, and she was made comfortable. Then the two returned to their seats at the front of the building, to smoke and chat a few minutes before retiring for the night.

CHAPTER XIII

A CONSULTATION

That mysterious warm-air current known as the Chinook wind steals through the depressions of the Rocky Mountains, at certain seasons of the year, from the mild surface of the Pacific, and tempers the severity of the winters in some portions of Montana, Wyoming, and the great West to a degree that renders them milder than many places farther south.

It was early in the month of May, when even in the Middle States it is not often comfortable to remain seated out of doors after the close of day, but Sterry and Whitney found it pleasant to occupy their chairs in front of the building, with no other protection then their own warm garments.

Whitney's wound was doing so well that he expressed himself ashamed to wear his arm in a sling. He freed it from the support, moved it readily about, and declared that after the next morning he would no longer shirk duty.

In one sense, Monteith Sterry was disappointed. He hoped they would be joined by Jennie, from whom he parted earlier in the evening, but he reflected that the hour was late, and she probably felt that her duty was with her sorrowing mother.

"She belongs there," he concluded, "and I respect her for doing her duty."

But she heard the murmur of voices after they had talked a few minutes, and appeared at the outer door, where she greeted her friend and listened with an intensity of interest that may be imagined to his account of his brush with the rustlers. Although she had become accustomed to danger during her life in the West, there could be no mistaking her solicitude for him. She said little, however, and, excusing herself, bade the two good-night.

"I tell you," said her brother, when she was gone, "if you stay, or rather attempt to stay, in this section, Mont, it is suicide—nothing more nor less."

"Well, I know times are likely to be warm, but, hang it, I can't bear the thought of being run out of Wyoming. It's a mighty big State, and there ought to be room enough for me."

"You persist in treating it lightly, but it is no trifling matter; you have been warned; were shot at, when we had our flurry with the rustlers; and, even while attempting to ride across the country, had the narrowest escape of your life—an escape so curious that it couldn't be repeated in a hundred years."

"It's the unexpected that happens."

"Not so often as the expected. Mont, what made you leave us so abruptly to-night?"

"O, I can hardly tell," replied the other, carelessly flinging one leg over the other and puffing at his cigar, as though the matter was of no importance.

"I know; you believed that if you stayed here you would increase the peril to us."

"You've hit it exactly; that was it."

"What sort of friends do you take us to be?"

"That isn't it; rather, what sort of friend would I be, thus knowingly to place you and your mother and sister in danger? If those rustlers knew where I am, a dozen would be here before sunrise."

"What of it? We are ready for them."

"That's a poor answer to my statement; you had enough of that woeful business yesterday; they hold me in such hatred that they would burn down your place, if they could reach me in no other way."

"And yet you propose to stay in Wyoming and have it out with them?"

"I haven't said that," remarked Sterry, more thoughtfully; "I may soon leave for a more civilized section, much as I hate to play the seeming coward; but what you said about my parents, brothers and sisters at home, gave me something to think over while riding across the prairie to-night."

"I shall hate to lose your company, for it is like old times to talk over our school days, but I would not be a friend to allow my selfishness to stand in the way of your good."

Sterry smoked a moment in silence, and then flung away his cigar and turned abruptly on his companion.

"Fred, if you could have prevented what took place yesterday by sacrificing every dollar of the property you have in Wyoming, you would have done it."

"Yes, God knows I would have done it a thousand times over; mother will never recover from the blow."

"And yet you may be the next to fall during this frightful state of affairs. If the situation of your mother and sister is so sad because of the loss of the head of the household, what will it be if you should be taken?"

"I appreciate your kindness, Mont, but you put the case too strongly; in one sense we all stand in danger of sudden death every day. I might live to threescore and ten in Wyoming, and be killed in a railroad accident or some other way the first day I left it. There is no particular enmity between the rustlers and me; that brush yesterday was one of those sudden outbursts that was not premeditated by them."

"It didn't look that way to me."

"You were not there when it opened. They were driving a lot of mavericks toward their ranch down the river, when Budd Hankinson saw a steer among them with our brand. You know it—a sort of cross with father's initials. Without asking for its return, Budd called them a gang of thieves, cut out the steer and drove him toward our range. If he had gone at the thing in the right way there would have been no trouble, but his ugly words made them mad, and the next thing we were all shooting at each other."

"You inflicted more harm than they, and they won't forget it."

"I don't want them to forget it," said Fred, bitterly, "but they won't carry their enmity to the extent of making an unprovoked attack on me or any of my people."

"Possibly not, but you don't want to bank on the theory."

"You must not forget," continued the practical Whitney, "that all we have in the world is invested in this business, and it would be a sacrifice for us to sell out and move eastward, where I would be without any business."

"You could soon make one for yourself."

"Well," said Whitney, thoughtfully, "I will promise to turn it over in my mind; the associations, however, that will always cling to this place, and particularly my sympathy for mother and Jennie, will be the strongest influences actuating me, provided I decide to change."

Mont Sterry experienced a thrill of delight, for he knew that when a man talks in that fashion he is on the point of yielding. He determined to urge the matter upon Jennie, and there was just enough hope in his heart that the prospect of being on the same side of the Mississippi with him would have some slight weight.

"I am glad to hear you speak thus, for it is certain there will be serious trouble with the rustlers."

"All which emphasizes what I said earlier in the evening about your duty to make a change of location."

The proposition, now that there was reason to believe that Fred Whitney had come over to his way of thinking, struck Sterry more favourably than before. In fact he reflected, with a shudder, what a dismal, unattractive section this would be, after the removal of his friends.

"I shall not forget your words; what you said has great influence with me, and you need not be surprised if I bid adieu to Wyoming within a week or a few days."

"It can't be too soon for your own safety, much as we shall regret to lose your company."

CHAPTER XIV

UNWELCOME CALLERS

Although Budd Hankinson and Grizzly Weber were removed from the scene of the events described, the night was not to pass without their becoming actors in some stirring incidents.

Ordinarily they would have spent the hours of darkness at the ranch of their employer, for the immense herds of cattle, as a rule, required no looking after. The ranges over which they grazed were so extensive that they were left to themselves, sometimes wandering for many miles from the home of their owner. They might not be seen for days and weeks. Their brands and the universal respect in which such proof of proprietorship was held prevented, as a rule, serious loss to the owners.

But the date will be recognized by the reader as one of a peculiarly delicate nature, when men were obliged to look more closely after their rights than usual.

The couple, therefore, rode behind the cattle to the foothills, along which they were expected to graze for an indefinite time. Hustlers were abroad, and the occurrences of the previous day had inflamed the feeling between them and the cowmen. It was not unlikely that, having been beaten off, some of them might take the means of revenging themselves by stealing a portion of the herd.

Budd and Weber dismounted after reaching the foothills, and, without removing the saddles from their horses, turned them loose to graze for themselves. No fear of their wandering beyond recall. A signal would bring them back the moment needed.

The hardy ranchers seated themselves with their backs against a broad, flat rock, which rose several feet above their heads. The bits were slipped from the mouths of their horses, so as to allow them to crop the succulent grass more freely, while the men gave them no attention, even when they gradually wandered beyond sight in the gloom.

"Times are getting lively in these parts," remarked Weber, as he filled his brierwood and lit it; "this thing can't go on forever; the rustlers or cowmen have got to come out on top, and I'm shot if one can tell just now which it will be."

"There can only be one ending," quietly replied his companion, whose pipe, being already lit, was puffed with the deliberate enjoyment of a veteran; "the rustlers may stir things up, and I s'pose they've got to get worse before they get better, but what's the use? It's like a mob or a riot; the scamps have things their own way at first, but they knuckle under in the end."

"I guess you're right; that was bad business yesterday; I shouldn't wonder if it ended in the young folks moving East again with their mother, whose heart is broke by the death of her husband."

"The younker is too plucky a chap to light out 'cause the governor has been sent under; he's had better luck than most tenderfeet who come out here and start in the cattle bus'ness; he done well last year, and if the rustlers let him alone, he'll do a good deal better this year; he may move, but he ain't agoin' to let them chaps hurry him, you can make up your mind to that."

The couple smoked a minute or two in silence. Then Weber, without removing his pipe from between his lips, uttered the words:

"Budd, something's going to happen powerful soon."

Hankinson, also keeping his pipe between his lips, turned his head and looked wonderingly at his friend. He did not speak, but the action told his curiosity; he did not understand the words.

"I mean what I say," added Weber, shaking his head; "I know it."

"What do you mean? Something happens every night and every day."

"That isn't what I'm driving at; something's going to happen afore daylight; you and me ain't through with this work."

Hankinson was still dissatisfied. He took his pipe from his mouth, and, looking sideways at his friend, asked:

"Can't you come down to facts and let a fellow know what you're driving at?"

"I don't exactly know myself, but I feel it in my left leg."

At this strange remark the other laughed heartily and silently. He had little patience with superstition. He knew his friend held peculiar whims in that respect. Weber expected something in the nature of scoffing and was prepared for it. He spoke doggedly:

"It has never deceived me. Six years ago, when we was trying to round up Geronimo and his Apache imps, ten of us camped in the Moggollon Mountains. Hot! Well, you never knowed anything like it. All day long the metal of our guns would blister our naked hands; we didn't get a drop of water from sunup till sundown; we was close on to the trail of the varmints, and we kept at it by moonlight till our horses gave out and we tumbled out among the rocks so used up that we could hardly stand. Our lieutenant was a bright young chap from South Car'lina that had come out of West Point only that summer, but he was true blue and warn't afeared of anything. We all liked him. I had seen him fight when a dozen of the Apaches thought they had us foul, and I was proud of him. He belonged to a good family, though that didn't make him any better than anyone else, but he treated us white.

"So when we went into camp, I goes to him and I says, says I, 'Lieutenant, there's going to be trouble.' He looked up at me in his pleasant way and asks, 'What makes you think so, Grizzly?' The others was listening, but I didn't mind that, and out with it. "Cause,' says I, 'my left leg tells me so.'"

"'And how does your leg tell you?' he asked again, with just a faint smile that wasn't anything like the snickers and guffaws of the other chaps. 'Whenever a twitch begins at the knee and runs down to my ankle,' says I, 'that is in the left leg, and then keeps darting back and forth and up and down, just as though some one was pricking it with a needle, do you know what it says?'"

"'I'm sure I don't, but I'd like to know.'"

Edward S. Ellis

"'Injins! Varmints! They're nigh you; look out!'"

"Wal, instead of j'ining the others in laughing at me, he says; just as earnest-like as if it was the colonel that had spoke, 'If that's the case, Grizzly, why we'll look out; you have been in this business afore I was born and I am glad you told me. I didn't s'pose any of 'em was within miles of us, but it's easy to be mistaken.'"

"Wal, to make a long story short we didn't any of us go to sleep; the boys laughed at what I said, but the way the lieutenant acted showed 'em he believed me, and that was enough. The Apaches come down on us that night and wiped out two of the boys. If the lieutenant hadn't showed his good sense by believing what I told him, there wouldn't have been one of us left."

Budd Hankinson then crossed his legs, extended on the ground as they were, shoved his sombrero back on his head, with his Winchester resting against the rock behind him, and smoked his pipe after the manner of a man who is pondering a puzzling question. The latter assumed much the same position, but, having said sufficient, was not disposed to speak until after the other had given his opinion.

"Grizzly, when your leg warns you like that, does it speak plain enough to tell you the sort of danger that's coming? Does it say what hour; where the trouble is to come from, and who them that make the trouble will be?"

"No!" replied the other, contemptuously; "how could a fellow's leg do that?"

"How could it do anything 'cept help tote him around when he wanted it to?"

"I've just explained, that twitching is a warning—that's all. I 'spose the leg thinks that's enough; so it is."

"There ain't any Apaches or Comanches in this part of the world."

"But there's rustlers, and where's the ch'ice?"

"Wal, Grizzly, all I've got to say is let 'em come; it ain't the first time we've seen 'em, and we're ginerally ready for 'em. We was yesterday, and I reckon we'll get there, all the same, to-night or to-morrow morning."

Grizzly Weber felt it his duty to be more explicit.

"The night I was telling you about down in Arizona wasn't the only time my leg signaled to me. While it allers means that something is going to come, it doesn't always mean it'll amount to much. It has happened that only a slight flurry follored. That may be the case to-night."

"What's to be done? Are we to set here on the ground and wait for it? I was going to take turns with you watching, but I guess we hadn't better go to sleep yet."

"You can sleep till near morning if you like, and when I want to lay down I'll wake you, but afore you do that I'll take a look around."

Weber rose to his feet, yawned, stretched his long, muscular arms, looked about him and listened. The moonlight enabled him to see only a comparatively short distance in any direction. Near-by were the forms of several cattle stretched upon the ground and sleeping. One or two were still chewing their cuds, but the scene was suggestive of rest and quiet, the reverse of what he told his friend was coming.

Edward S. Ellis

The horses had drifted too far off to be visible, but it was certain they were within signal distance. Rocks, stunted undergrowth, bushes, and the rich, luxuriant grass met the eye everywhere. Thousands of cattle were scattered over an area of many acres, and, unless molested by dishonest persons, would be within ready reach when the time for the round-up arrived. Neither eye nor ear could detect anything of the peril which the rancher believed impended with the same faith that he believed the sun would rise on the following morning.

That faith could not be shaken by the profound quiet. Without speaking again to his friend he strolled toward the north, that is parallel with the spur along whose slope the cattle were grazing. As he moved forward they were continually in sight. Most of them were lying on the ground, but a few were on their feet, browsing and acquiring the luscious plumpness which has made that section one of the most famous grazing regions of the Union. They paid no attention to the rancher while making his way around, among and past them. They were too accustomed to the sight of the sturdy cattleman to be disturbed by him.

An eighth of a mile from the rock where he had left his comrade, Weber once more paused. Nothing as yet had come to confirm that peculiar warning described, but his faith knew no weakening on that account.

From a long way came the sound of rifle-firing, sometimes rapid, and sometimes consisting of dropping shots.

"They're at it somewhere," muttered the rancher; "it doesn't come from the ranch, so I guess the folks are all right."

The reports were too far off for him to feel any interest in them; that which was foretold by the twitching of his limb must come much closer to answer the demands of the occasion.

Weber resumed his walk around and among the prostrate animals. He was on the alert, glancing to the right and left, and speculating as to the nature of the "trouble" that could not be far off.

Through the impressive stillness he caught a subdued sound which caused him again to stop in his walk and listen. His keen vision could discover nothing, nor was he certain of the nature of the disturbance.

He knelt down and pressed his ear to the ground. That told the story; several hundred of the herd were in motion and moving away from him. They would not do this of their own accord, and the rancher translated its meaning at once; they were being driven off.

He broke into a loping trot toward the threatened point, holding his Winchester ready for instant use. As he was likely to need his horse, he placed his fingers between his lips and emitted the whistle by which he was accustomed to summon the faithful beast. Then he sent out a different call. That was for the listening ears of Budd Hankinson, who would be sure to hasten to his comrade.

But Weber did not wait for man or animal. They could come as fast as they chose. The case was too urgent to admit of delay.

He believed the moving cattle were hardly a furlong distant, but they were not only going at a rapid pace, but were moving directly away from where the rancher had halted.

He could run as swiftly and as long as an Indian, but the

Edward S. Ellis

course was difficult, and he believed the cattle were going so fast that he was gaining little if anything on them. When he had run a short way he stopped and glanced impatiently back in the gloom.

"Why doesn't Cap hurry?" he muttered, referring to his horse; "he must have heard my call, and he never lets it pass him. Budd, too, don't want to break his neck trying to overtake me."

His impatience made him unjust. Neither man nor beast had had time to come up, even though each had set out at their best speed the moment they heard the signal. They would be on hand in due course, unless prevented.

Weber called them again, with a sharp, peremptory signal, which could not fail to apprise both of the urgency of the case. Then, afraid of losing any advantage, he pushed after the fleeing cattle. The figures of the sleeping animals around him grew fewer in number. By and by none was to be seen. He had passed the outer boundary of those that were left, and was now tramping over the section from which they had been stampeded or driven by the rustlers.

He dropped to the ground again. But it was only to use the earth as a medium of hearing. The multitudinous trampings became distinct once more. The cattle were running, proof that the thieves were pressing them hard and were in fear of pursuit.

Leaping up again, the rancher peered backward in the moonlight. Something took shape, and he identified the figure of a man approaching. The Winchester was grasped and half aimed, so as to be ready for instant use.

But it was his friend, who was coming on the run. Budd

Hankinson had heard the call, and obeyed it with surprising promptness.

"What's up?" he asked, as he halted, breathing not a whit faster because of his unusual exertion.

"They're running off some of the cattle; where's the hosses?"

"Hanged if I know! I called to Dick the minute I started, but he didn't show up; I don't know were he is."

"I whistled for Cap at the same time I did for you; he ought to be here first. I wonder if they've stolen him?" added Weber, affrightedly.

"No, they wouldn't have come that close; they didn't have the chance; but it gets me."

With that he sent out the signal once more. Budd did the same, and then they broke into their swift, loping trot after the fleeing animals, both in an ugly mood.

They were at great disadvantage without their own horses when it was clear the rustlers were mounted. But, though on foot, the ranchers could travel faster than the gait to which the cattle had been forced. They increased their speed, and it was quickly evident they were gaining on the rogues.

It was not long before they discerned the dark bodies galloping off in alarm. Almost at the same moment the ranchers saw the outlines of two horsemen riding from right to left, and goading the cattle to an injuriously high pace. Grizzly Weber, who was slightly in advance, turned his head and said, in excitement:

"Budd, they're not rustlers; they're Injins!"

Edward S. Ellis

CHAPTER XV

THE "DOG INDIANS"

Weber was right in his declaration that the parties who were stampeding a part of the herd were Indians. They were two in number, both superbly mounted, and dashing back and forth with great swiftness, as they urged the animals to a frantic flight. They knew the danger of pursuit and the value of time.

The rancher, who shouted to his companion, was a few paces in advance at the exciting moment he made the discovery. The sight so angered him that he stopped abruptly and brought his rifle to his shoulder, with the intention of shooting the marauder from his horse.

This would have been done the next instant but for the exclamation of Grizzly Weber. Despite the noise and confusion, the Indian heard him and saw his danger. Before the rancher could sight his weapon the thief seemed to plunge headlong over the further side of his steed; but instead of doing so he resorted to the common trick of his people, all of whom are unsurpassable horsemen. He flung himself so far over that nothing of his body remained visible. The horse himself became the shield between him and the white man. The redskin was in the saddle, but he would have been just as expert had he been riding bareback.

Weber muttered his disappointment, but held his rifle ready to fire the instant he caught sight of any part of the fellow's person. At any rate, a recourse was open to him; he could shoot the horse, and thus place his enemy on the same footing with himself. He decided to do so.

The hurly-burly was bewildering. The cattle were bellowing in affright, galloping frenziedly before the two horsemen, dashing back and forth among them at the rear like two lunatics, and goading them to desperate haste.

At the instant the Indian whom Grizzly Weber selected as his man eluded his fatal aim, his horse was running diagonally. This could not be continued without the abandonment of the herd. He must wheel, to come back behind the fleeing cattle. The rancher waited for that moment, prepared to fire the instant any tangible part of the body of the rogue was revealed by the moonlight.

But an astonishing exploit prevented the shot. The savage wheeled, just as was anticipated, but, in the act of doing so, threw himself for a second time over the side of his horse, so as to interpose his body. He did it with such inimitable dexterity that the rancher was baffled.

All this took place in a twinkling, as may be said; but, brief as was the time, it caused Weber to lose valuable ground. The horse was growing dimmer in the gloom, and, unless checked, would quickly be beyond reach of the Winchester still levelled at him. Nothing was easier than to drive a bullet through his brain and then have it out with the Indian. Possibly the single bullet would end the career of both.

Budd Hankinson called out something, but Grizzly Weber

did not catch it. With grim resolution he sighted as best he could in the moonlight at the galloping steed, and then with a shiver lowered his weapon undischarged, awed by the sudden discovery of the deed he had come within a hair of committing.

The erratic motions of the Indian and his horse entangled both with the flying cattle. All at once the nimble steed became so crowded on every side that his only escape from being gored to death was by a tremendous bound which he made over the back of a terrified steer who lowered his head for the purpose of driving his horns into his body. He made the leap with amazing skill and grace.

As he went up in the air, with the Indian clinging to his side, the astonishing leap was executed with perfect ease, precision and perfectness, his figure rising above the mass of struggling animals and standing out for a moment in clear relief.

That one glimpse of the outlines of the splendid horse, together with the brilliancy of the performance itself, told Grizzly Weber that the steed was his own Cap. The owner had by a hair escaped sending a bullet through the brain of the animal whom he loved as his own brother.

Grizzly was stupefied for an instant. Then, knowing that Cap had been duped by some conjuration, he sent out the familiar signal with a sharp distinctness that rose above the din and racket, which, to ordinary ears, would have been overwhelming.

The result was remarkable, and approached the ridiculous. Cap heard the call, and instantly turned to obey it. The Indian on his back strove furiously to prevent and to keep him at his work. Cap fought savagely, flinging his head aloft, rearing, plunging, and refusing to follow the direction toward which the redskin twisted his head by sheer strength. It was a strife between rider and steed, and the latter made no progress in either direction while keeping up the fight, which was as fierce as it was brief.

The Indian could not force the horse to obey him, and the efforts of Cap to reach his master were defeated by the wrenching at the bit. It looked as if the horse had been seized with the frenzy that possessed every one, and was fighting and struggling aimlessly and accomplishing nothing.

But Grizzly Weber was not the one to stand idly by and allow this extraordinary contest to go on. Nothing intervened between him and the daring marauder, and he dashed toward him.

The redskin's audacity, nimbleness and self-possession excited the admiration of Grizzly Weber, angered though he was at the trick played on him. The rider knew the risk of keeping up the fight with the obdurate beast, for the master was sure to arrive on the spot within a few seconds. Before the rancher could reach him he went from the saddle as if shot out of a gun.

Freed from his incubus, Cap emitted a joyful whinny and trotted toward his master.

"You rascal!" exclaimed the delighted rancher, vaulting upon his back in a twinkling. "Now we'll settle with the chap that tried to part you and me."

All this consumed but a few moments. The Indian could not have gone far. He would not dash among the cattle, who, now that they were stampeded, were as dangerous as so many wild beasts. He had hardly time to conceal himself,

Edward S. Ellis

and Grizzly was certain that he had him.

All the same, however, the cowman made a miscalculation. When he wheeled Cap about to run down the daring redskin he was nowhere to be seen. There were no trees near, but there were boulders, rocks and depressions, with the rich grass everywhere, and the dusky thief was as safe as if beyond the Assinaboine, in British territory.

"I'm glad of it," thought Weber, a moment later; "a redskin that can show such a performance as that desarves to save his scalp."

In the dizzying flurry Grizzly had no time to think of his companion, who had enough to attend to his own matters. He now looked around for him, but he, too, was invisible.

"I wonder whether he got his horse back, for Dick must have been stole, the same as was Cap."

And, grateful for having regained possession of his horse, he patted the silken neck of the noble animal.

Grizzly's years of experience with cattle apprised him of a gratifying truth. The course of the stampeded herd was changing. Instead of fleeing away from the main body they were veering around, so that, if the change of course continued, they would return to the neighbourhood from which they started.

Panic-smitten cattle are not apt to do a thing of that kind of their own accord. Some cause, and a strong one, too, must have effected this diversion in the line of flight. All at once, above the din, sounded the penetrating voice of a man, who was striving with herculean energy to change the course of the wild animals.

One sound of that voice was sufficient to identify it as Budd Hankinson's. He must have played his cards well to have done all this in so brief a space of time.

And such had been the case beyond a doubt. Budd suspected from the first what did not enter Grizzly's mind until it flashed upon him as described. The fact that neither of their horses appeared when summoned convinced Budd that they had been stolen. True, even in that case they would have obeyed the signal, had they been near enough, and had the circumstances allowed them to identify it; but, although not far off, the noise immediately around them shut out the call of Grizzly from their ears, until he repeated it, as has been told.

Hankinson anticipated his friend in this act. In his case, the thief in the saddle of Dick gave it up at once. He leaped off, and whisked out of sight. It was then Budd called to Grizzly that the thieves had their horses; but the other did not catch his words, and, therefore, gave them no further heed.

The instant Budd's feet were in the stirrups he set his horse bounding along the side of the herd, with the purpose of checking the stampede by changing its course. Grizzly understood matters and set off after him, leaving to the sagacious Cap to thread his way to the other side of the running cattle.

In the course of a few minutes the ranchers opened communication and pushed their work with a vigor which brought good results. The cattle were tired. They had been on their feet most of the day while grazing, were growing fat, and naturally were indisposed to severe exertion. Their pace dropped to a walk, and sooner than would have been supposed, the fright passed off. The herders kept them moving until close to the main herd, where they were allowed to rest. Budd and Grizzly dismounted once more, turning their horses loose, and seated themselves on the ground. The night, as will be remembered, was mild, and they did not need their blankets to make them comfortable.

"Wal," was the smiling remark of Grizzly, as he began refilling his pipe, "my leg didn't deceive me this time."

"No, I'll own up it played square; but, Grizzly, if we've got to fight the red varmints as well as rustlers, there will be some lively fun in Wyoming and Montana before the thing is over."

"The Injins won't take a hand in this. You know who them two thieves were, don't you?"

"A couple of 'dog Injins,' of course."

"There isn't anybody else that's got anything to do with this; it's sort of queer—that is, it has struck me so two or three times—that the Injins have tramps among 'em the same as white folks. They call 'em 'dog Injins,' I s'pose, 'cause they don't claim any particular tribe, but tramp back and forth over the country, slipping off their reservations whenever they get a chance."

"Yes, there are plenty of 'em," assented Budd; "we've met 'em before; you'll find 'em as far north as the Saskatchewan and as low down as the Rio Grande. But I say, Grizzly, they were two slick ones; I never seen finer work."

"Nor me either; if they had been satisfied with taking our hosses we'd never seen 'em agin. Gracious!" added the rancher, "for myself, I'd rather lost half the herd than Cap."

"It seems to me," said Budd, after smoking a moment in

silence, "that although them 'dog Injins' was pretty smart in getting out of the way when we come down on 'em, they weren't smart in trying to run off the cattle. They must have known we'd find it out at daylight and would be after 'em hot-footed."

Grizzly had been puzzling over the same phase of the question. The 'dog Indian' is a vagabond, who, belonging to some particular tribe, as of necessity must be the case, affiliates with none, but goes whithersoever his will leads him, provided he is not prevented. Sometimes they remain on the reservation for weeks and months, as orderly, industrious and well-behaved as the best of the red men. Then they disappear, and may not turn up for a long time. In truth, they are as likely not to turn up at all, but to lead their wandering, useless lives just as the vagrants do in civilized communities.

Surely the couple who had played their parts in the incidents of the night must have known that nothing could be gained by stampeding a part of Whitney's herd. The cattle were branded, and could not be disposed of for that reason. Besides, a couple of Indians in charge of several hundred cattle would be objects of suspicion themselves, and certain to be called to account. They could make no common cause with the rustlers, for the latter would have naught to do with them.

More than likely Grizzly Weber hit the truth when he said:

"It was a piece of pure deviltry on their part. When they got into the saddles they felt safe. Instead of making off with the hosses, they thought they would stir up a little fun by stampeding the cattle. After injuring 'em by rapid driving for a good many miles they would have paid no more attention to 'em, and let us find 'em as best we could."

Edward S. Ellis

"Yes," assented Budd, "they bit off more'n they could chaw, and so lost the hosses. But, Grizzly, have you noticed there's been several guns shot off around the country to-night?"

"Yas," replied the other, indifferently; "I've heard 'em several times, but I haven't obsarved any coming from the house; it must be that some of the boys are having fun to-night instead of sleeping like lambs, as they ought to do."

"And there'll be more of it to-morrow, but that's what we've got to expect at all times. I'm going to sleep; call me when you want me."

Budd spread the blanket, which he had taken from the back of his horse, on the ground and lay down. Hardly five minutes passed when he was wrapped in sound slumber. To prevent himself from becoming unconscious, Grizzly rose and walked slowly around and among the herd. He had no thought of anything further occurring, for the 'dog Indians' would be certain to keep away from that neighbourhood after what had occurred. He did not feel easy, however, concerning his friends at the ranch. He knew trouble was at hand, and he would have been glad if the mother and daughter were removed beyond danger. The sounds of rifle-firing and the bright glow in the horizon, made by a burning building, confirmed his misgivings as to what a few days or hours were sure to bring forth.

CHAPTER XVI

AN UNPLEASANT VISIT

IT will be recalled that during these incidents Monteith Sterry and Fred Whitney were sitting at the front of the long, low building, which was the home of the latter, discussing the incidents of the last day or two, as well as the matter of Whitney removing, with his family, to the East, in order to prevent any addition to the affliction they had just suffered.

Besides this, Whitney had turned on his young friend, and impressed upon him that he, too, was incurring unjustifiable risk by remaining in Wyoming during the inflamed state of public feeling. There was much less excuse in the case of Sterry than of his host. He ought to be at home prosecuting the study of his profession, as his parents wished him to do. His health was fully restored, and it cannot be denied that he was wasting his precious days. He was fond of his father, mother, brothers and sisters, and it would grieve them beyond expression if he should uselessly sacrifice himself.

"Yes," he replied, "I cannot deny the truth of what you say, Fred. I ought to leave this part of the country."

"Of course; you're not needed; your future has been mapped for you, and it is hard to make up lost time."

"We found that out at the high school," returned Mont, with a light laugh; "but the pearl of great price, in a worldly sense, is good health, and I have been repaid in securing it."

"And having secured it, it remains—Mont," added his companion abruptly, but without the slightest change of tone, "don't stop to ask me why, but step quickly through the door and into the house, and keep out of sight for a few minutes."

"I understand," said Sterry, obeying without an instant's hesitation.

The prompt, unquestioning compliance with the request of Fred Whitney showed that Monteith Sterry understood the reason that it was made of him.

The truth was, that during the last few minutes the young men were talking in front of the house, each descried something suspicious on the broad plain. They instinctively lowered their voices, and though neither made reference to it, both gave more attention to it than to their own words.

They heard nothing of the tramp of horses, but saw the shadowy figures of several men hovering on what may be termed the line of invisibility. Sometimes they were distinguished quite clearly, and then seemed to vanish; but the youths could not be mistaken.

A number of persons were out there, not mounted, but on foot, and moving about, without approaching any closer, for the space of several minutes. It looked as if they were reconnoitering the house from a distance and debating the best manner of procedure.

The suspicions of the friends were the same. They were rustlers looking for the inspector.

Mont Sterry would have preferred to stay where he was and have it out with them, but the circumstances were so peculiar that he could not refuse to do as his comrade requested.

The cause of Whitney's wish was the abrupt increasing distinctness of the figures, proof that they had reached a decision and were approaching the house.

They speedily came into plain sight, four men, in the garb of cowmen, and they were rustlers beyond question.

Conscious that they were seen, they now advanced directly, as if coming from a distance, though the fact that they were on foot showed that such was not the case.

With feelings which it would be hard to describe, Fred Whitney recognized the first as Larch Cadmus, wearing the same whiskers as before. Had he been thoughtful enough to disguise his voice the young man would not have suspected his identity.

The moon had worked around into that quarter of the heavens that its light shone on the figure of Fred, who rose to his feet, as was his custom, and advanced a few paces to meet the newcomers.

"Good evening!" he said. "How happens it that you are afoot at this time of night?"

"Our horses ain't fur off," replied Cadmus; "the rest of the boys didn't think it worth while to trouble you."

"What do you mean by troubling me?" asked Fred, though he understood the meaning.

"We're on an unpleasant errand," continued Cadmus, acting

as the spokesman of the party, the others remaining in the background and maintaining silence.

"Shall I bring chairs for you? It is so unusually mild to-night that I am sitting out doors from choice, and I do not wish to disturb my mother and sister, who retired some time ago."

"No, we'll stand," was the curt response. "Whitney, as I suppose it is, are you accustomed to sit out here alone?"

"Not when I can have company."

"Were you alone before we came up?"

"When you were here earlier in the evening, as you saw for yourself, I had my sister and a friend."

"Exactly; who was that friend?"

"Mont Sterry, the gentleman who is on a little tour through some parts of Wyoming and Montana to try to help make you fellows behave yourselves."

"Yes; wal, we're looking for him."

"Why do you come here?"

"Because he spends a good deal of his time here; he seems to be interested in Miss Whitney."

"Well, if he is, that is no business of yours," retorted Fred, angered by the reference to his sister.

"Perhaps not, but it would be well for you to keep a civil tongue in your head, Fred Whitney; we're not in a pleasant mood to-night, for we've had trouble."

"It matters not to me what trouble you've had; you have no right to name any member of my family. They are in affliction; my father was shot down by your gang yesterday, and, though we made several of you fellows bite the dust, the whole of them weren't worth his little finger."

"We'll let them matters drop; I told you we're looking for Mont Sterry, and we're going to have him."

"And I ask you again, why do you come here after him? I don't deny that he was with me, but he left fully two hours ago."

"We know that; he gave us the slip, but we believe he came back."

"And I ask what reason you have for such belief; why did he bid us good-by and ride away? I know that he had not the slightest intention of returning for several days," said Fred, sticking to the technical truth.

"We don't care what his intention was, he did come back."

"How do you know that?"

"He was sitting in that chair alongside of you less than ten minutes ago; you were smoking and talking, though you didn't speak loud enough for us to catch your words."

"Where is the proof, Larch Cadmus, of what you say?"

Without noticing this penetration of his disguise, the rustler turned and spoke to the nearest of his companions:

"Spark Holly, how was it?"

"I seen 'em both and heard 'em talking," was the prompt response of the individual appealed to.

"Are your eyes better than the others'?" asked Fred.

"They don't have to be," replied Cadmus, speaking for him. "While we stayed in front of the house, Spark stole round to the rear, where none of your family seen him. He got to the corner and had a good look at both of you."

"Does he know Sterry?" inquired Fred, purposely raising his voice, that his friend, standing a few feet away within the house, should not miss a word.

"He don't know him, but I do, and the description Spark gives fits the man we're after to a T. We want him."

"But the notice you gave Sterry allowed him twenty-four hours' grace. Why do you ask for him now?"

"Them was my sentiments, but when I joined the party under Inman, a little while ago, he told me the boys had reconsidered that matter, and decided that after what Sterry has done, and tried to do, I hadn't any right to make the promise."

"That may be their decision, but it cannot affect yours; you are bound by the pledge you made in writing to him."

Larch Cadmus, like his companions, was growing impatient. He said:

"I haven't come here to argue the matter with you; I've come after my man, and am going to have him."

"And I repeat what I said: he left more than two hours ago, and you have no business to come here."

"Do you mean to tell me he isn't in the house?" demanded Cadmus, with rising temper.

"I refuse to answer, but I do say that neither you nor any of your gang shall enter my home, where are my mother and sister, their hearts stricken by your murderous doings of yesterday, except over my dead body."

"We don't like to disturb the ladies," said Cadmus, "but we mean business; we have promised the boys to bring back that fellow; but I'll make a proposition."

"What is it?"

"If you will say that Mont Sterry is not in there, we'll go away without disturbing any one; we'll take your word."

"I recognize no right of yours to question me," was the scornful reply of Fred Whitney.

"Boys," said Cadmus, turning again to his companions, "that's only another way of owning up that the coward is hiding here, afraid to meet us; he's our game."

Edward S. Ellis

CHAPTER XVII

A DELICATE SITUATION

Few men possessed more courage than Fred Whitney, and he was thoroughly aroused.

Sitting in front of his own home during the evening, it naturally happened that he was without any weapon at immediate command. His Winchester and revolvers, his inseparable companions, during those stirring times, whenever away from home, were inside. It need not be said that every one of the rustlers had his "guns" in his possession, so he was a single, defenceless man against four armed ones.

Nevertheless, he strode forward in front of the open door, determined to make good his threat.

"You talk of cowards," he said; "you are four, and each has his pistols and rifle; I have none and one arm is wounded, but I defy you!"

"Come, come," said the leader, "this will do you no good; we're bound to have that man, and if he won't come out we must go after him. If you stand in the way we'll pitch you aside. We don't want to hurt you."

"Advance at your peril—"

"Fred, move a little to the left—that will do. I've got a bead on him now."

It was the voice of Mont Sterry, a few feet away, in the darkness of the room. The muzzle of his rifle, however, projected just enough to reflect the moonlight, and it was leveled at the breast of Larch Cadmus.

"One step," added Sterry, "and you're a dead man."

"Larch Cadmus," said Fred, thrilled by the occurrence, "for we recognize you despite those whiskers, I never knew Mont Sterry to break his word!"

Language cannot do justice to the situation. At the very moment the miscreant was about to advance to hurl Whitney from his path he was confronted by the muzzle of a loaded rifle, held by a man who was in deadly earnest, and who realized he was at bay.

The startled ruffian recoiled a step and stared into the darkened room, as if he failed to grasp the situation.

"Not a step in any direction," said Sterry, warningly; "if you attempt to retreat, advance, or move aside, I'll fire."

It would be a rash thing for any one to deny that the young inspector had secured the "drop" on Larch Cadmus.

But the man was accustomed to violence, and it took him but a minute to rally.

"Pretty well done, I'll own," he said, with a forced laugh; "but what good is it going to do you? There are three more of us here and a half-dozen hardly a hundred yards away."

"And what good will they do you?"

"Spark," said Cadmus, "slip back to the boys and give 'em the tip; we'll see about this thing."

"The moment Spark or either of the other two stirs I'll let the moonlight through *you!* I'm going to keep my gun pointed right at you, Mr. Cadmus. If those fellows think I'm worth more than you, they have a chance to prove it, for only one of them has to take the first step to leave, when I'll press this trigger just a little harder than now. More than that, if one of them shouts, whistles, or makes any kind of a signal, I'll do as I threaten. If any man doesn't think so, let him make the trial."

"Well, I'll be hanged!" muttered Larch Cadmus; "this *is* a go!"

Judging from the new turn of affairs, it looked as if a single individual had the "drop" on four others.

It struck Larch Cadmus that this was a good occasion for something in the nature of a compromise.

"See here, Sterry," he said, assuming an affected jocularity which deceived no one, "I'll own you've played it on me mighty fine. But you can't stand there all night with your Winchester p'inted at me, and bime-by I'll git tired; can't we fix the matter up some way?"

"Fred," said Sterry, with the same coolness shown from the first, "slip through the door; you know where your gun is; stoop a little, so I won't have to shift my aim; when that is done we'll talk about compromise."

Fred Whitney, as quick as his companion to "catch on," did instantly what was requested. He dodged into the darkened apartment, with which, of course, he was so familiar that he needed the help of no light to find his weapon.

Had Larch Cadmus been as subtle as his master, perhaps he might have prevented this by ordering one of his men to cover Whitney with his gun, though it is more than probable that Sterry still would have forced the leading rustler to his own terms.

But there was one among the four with the cunning of a fox; he was Spark Holly, who had located the inspector when in front of the house.

At the moment Cadmus was brought up all standing, as may be said, Holly stood so far to one side that he was not in the young man's field of vision. He, like his two companions, could have slipped off at any moment without danger to himself, but it would have been at the cost of their leader's life; nor could they shift their position and raise a weapon to fire into the room, where there was a prospect of hitting the daring youth at bay, without precipitating that catastrophe.

The instant, however, Fred Whitney turned his back on the rustlers, Holly saw his opportunity. He vanished.

The others, more sluggish than he, held their places, dazed, wondering, stupefied, and of no more account than so many logs of wood.

Shrewd enough to do this clever thing, Spark Holly was too cautious to spoil it by allowing his movement to be observed. Had he darted over the plain in front of the house, Mont Sterry would have seen the fleeing figure, understood what it meant, and, carrying out his threat, shot down Larch Cadmus.

Edward S. Ellis

Holly lost no time in dodging behind the structure, moving with the stealth of an Indian in the stillness of the night. Then he made a circuit so wide that, as he gradually described a half-circle and came round to the point whence he had first advanced to the dwelling, he was so far off that the keenest vision from the interior could not catch a glimpse of him.

Certain of this, he ran only a short distance, when he came up with the half-dozen mounted rustlers of whom Cadmus had spoken, and who were wondering at the unaccountable delay.

The messenger quickly made everything plain, and they straightway proceeded to take a hand in the business.

CHAPTER XVIII

A MISCALCULATION

Larch Cadmus was well fitted to act the leader of so desperate a company of men. He was chagrined beyond measure at the manner in which the tables had been turned on him, but, like all such persons, when caught fairly, he knew how to accept the situation philosophically.

None understood better than he that the individual who held that Winchester levelled would press the trigger on the first provocation. He was the one that had sent the warning, and the other was the one that had received it. The twenty-four hours' truce had been ended by the words and action of Cadmus himself, and his chief wonder, now that Fred Whitney was with him, was that Monteith Sterry should show any mercy to his persecutor; had the situations been reversed, the course also would have been different.

But the ruffian was on the alert. He noticed the guarded movement of Spark Holly at the moment Whitney entered his home, and he needed no one to tell him what it meant.

He had slipped off to bring help and it would not take him long to do it, though Cadmus might well feel uneasy over what would take place when Sterry should learn the trick

Edward S. Ellis

played on him.

It may be that a person's senses are keener in situations of grave peril than at other times, for, calculating as clearly as he could the period it would take his comrade to reach the horsemen, only a short way back on the prairie, Cadmus heard sounds which indicated their approach, though they must remain invisible for several minutes.

"Wal," said he, in his off-hand manner, directly after Whitney had whisked into the house, "now that you're together, how long do you mean to keep this thing up?"

"We're through," was the response.

"What do you mean?" asked the surprised fellow.

"You can go away as soon as you please. Mont Sterry doesn't care anything more about you, but I'll keep you covered as long as you are in sight, and if you or any of your men try any deception you'll take the consequences."

With a moment's hesitation, doubtless caused by distrust of his master, Cadmus began edging to one side. A few steps were enough to take him out of range of that dreaded weapon, and then his demeanour changed.

"That was a good trick of yours, Mont Sterry, but it won't do you a bit of good."

"Why not?"

"Here come the rest of the boys, and if you think you can hold them up, why try it."

At that moment the horsemen assumed form in the gloom

and approached the house in a diagonal direction. Encouraged by their presence, Larch Cadmus once more moved toward the open door and resumed the position of leader.

"Now, my fine fellow, we summon you to surrender," he called in his brusquest voice and manner.

The reply was striking. A young man stepped from the door and advanced to meet the horsemen. There was an instant when Cadmus believed his victim had come forth to give himself up as commanded, but one glance showed that it was Fred Whitney. He calmly awaited the coming of the mounted men, saluted them, and said:

"You have come for Mont Sterry, and Cadmus there assures me that if I give him my word that he is not in my house he will accept the statement; do you agree to it?"

"How's that, Larch?" asked Ira Inman, turning toward him.

"Them was my words, but—"

"Well, then, I have to say that Mont Sterry is not in my house; the only persons there are my mother and sister."

"But I seen him, and he got the drop on me—how's that?"

"Yes," replied Whitney, enjoying his triumph, "he was there a few minutes ago, and he *did* get the drop on you and the rest of your fellows; but I took his place; he went out of the back door, mounted his mare, and if there's any of you that think you can overhaul him, you can't start a moment too soon."

No man who heard these words doubted their truth. They told such a straightforward tale that they could not be questioned.

They would have been zanies had they believed that, with the back door at command and the certain approach of his enemies, Sterry had waited for them to attack him.

True, he and his friend would have held a strong position, in which they could have made it warm for the others, but the ultimate advantage must have been on the side of the assailants.

The laugh was on Cadmus, and those were the men who, in their chagrin, vented their feelings upon him. The worst of it was, he was as angry as they; but he might well ask how he could have helped himself, and whether any one of them would have done any better.

The foxy Holly, at a whispered word from Inman, darted around the end of the building and entered the stables. A brief examination showed that no animals, all being known to him, except those belonging to Whitney, were there.

Had any doubt remained, it was removed by his sense of hearing. Without the intervention of the dwelling to obstruct the sound, he caught the faint, rhythmic beating of the earth, barely audible and gradually growing fainter in the distance. It was just such a sound as is made by a horse going at a leisurely, sweeping gallop, and that was the explanation he gave it.

Mont Sterry was safe beyond pursuit, for there was no horse in the company that could overtake him. Spark Holly returned to the party in front and made his report.

It may be said the report was accepted and placed on file for future reference.

It was characteristic of those men, too, that they did not

delay their own actions, now that their business may be said to have been finished.

"Well," said Inman, "that isn't the first time that fellow gave us the slip to-night. The way he did it before was mighty clever, but I don't see that he deserves any credit for fooling Cadmus, for any one would have known enough to do that. But remember that Mr. Mont Sterry is still in Wyoming, and we are not through with him yet."

"And there ain't any twenty-four hours' truce," added Cadmus.

"After what has taken place, there's little fear of Sterry making any mistake on that point," said Whitney, who was so pleased over the outcome of matters that he could speak in gentler terms than he would have used had the circumstances been different.

It would seem strange that these men, who but a brief time before were so hostile to the single person now in their power, should converse without the least offensive action; but most, if not all, of the doings of the men concerned in the late troubles in that section were in hot blood, and would not have occurred had time been taken for thought and consideration.

Inman and his brother rustlers wheeled about and rode off in the direction whence they came. Their movements indicated that they had no intention of following Sterry, since the course taken by him was almost directly the opposite; but Whitney was not fully satisfied. He remained in front of his home, listening in the stillness of the night to the sounds made by the hoofs of the galloping horses.

Gradually they grew fainter, until, had there been any air

stirring, or had the tension of hearing been less, he would have heard nothing; but, when the noises were hovering close to inaudibility, they continued thus. They neither increased nor diminished, but remaining the same, steadily shifted the direction whence they came.

Instead of keeping to the westward, as they had been for a long time, they worked around to the north and east. Then the decrease in distinctness of sound was so rapid that it was quickly lost.

The truth was evident: the rustlers had started in pursuit of Sterry, though why they should have taken so much pains to conceal the fact from Fred Whitney was more than he could understand.

"They may overtake him," thought the young man as he turned to enter the house, "but it will not be right away."

A light foot-fall sounded in the darkness of the room.

"Is that you, Jennie?" he asked in a guarded undertone.

"Yes, brother; have they gone?"

"Some time ago. Is mother asleep?"

"She was asleep before they came, utterly worn out. I am glad she knows nothing of the cause of their visit. And what of Monteith?"

"He is many miles away, and still riding hard."

"Will they pursue him?"

"Let them do so if they wish, they will have a fine time

overtaking him," was the light reply of the brother, who, leaning over in the gloom, affectionately kissed his sister good-night.

Edward S. Ellis

CHAPTER XIX

THE BURNED RANCH

Meanwhile Monteith Sterry was making the best of his opportunity.

It was no great exploit for him to slip out of the back door, when he found his enemies gathering in front; but, had he not been convinced that the movement was in the interests of his friends, as well as himself, he would not have made it.

His flight was at a moderate pace for several hundred yards, by which time he considered himself safe from pursuit and gave his mare free rein. Her speed was rapid, but she was capable of maintaining it for hours without fatigue.

Sterry's intention was to make his way to the ranch of his friend, Dick Hawkridge, which lay to the westward. He began veering in that direction, so that it may be said that while Inman and his band were riding toward him, he was approaching them. Two causes, however, prevented a meeting of the parties.

Sterry was much further out than the rustlers, and in the darkness they could see nothing, if indeed they could hear anything of each other. Then he had not ridden far when he was checked by an unexpected sight.

A bright red glow appeared to the northward in the sky. It was too vivid, distinct and near for him to mistake its nature. It was a burning building, the flames showing so strongly that, aware as he was of the deceptive nature of such a light, he knew it was no more than a mile away. He turned the head of his mare in that direction.

"Things seem to be stirring to-night," was his thought as he galloped forward, with his gaze fixed on the burning structure. "That may be an accident, but such accidents are not common in this part of the world."

His supposition was that it was the work of the rustlers, but he was mistaken.

The building was similar to that occupied by the Whitneys, though somewhat smaller, and burned so fast that when he reached the spot it was a mass of blazing embers, with hardly a semblance of the original structure remaining.

The sight was interesting of itself, but the attention of Sterry was riveted by the figure of a man lying motionless on the ground, only a few paces in front of where the door had been. His nerveless right hand still grasped the Winchester with which he had evidently made a sturdy fight when stricken down.

Sterry did not dismount, but, sitting in the saddle, looked on the sorrowful sight as revealed by the glow of the burning building. He was saddened that such things should be.

Little time, however, was given him for gloomy reverie, when Queenie sniffed the air and turned her head a little to one side. Looking in that direction, the rider saw the figure

Edward S. Ellis

of a horseman assume shape in the glow as his animal advanced at a slow step. He must have detected Sterry before the latter saw him, and was studying him with close attention, his rifle supported across his saddle in front, ready for instant use.

Reading his suspicion, the young man called out:

"Come on, partner! You and I cannot be enemies at such a time as this."

The salutation reassured the other, who increased his pace.

Before he reached Sterry the latter half-regretted his action, for he recognized the man as Duke Vesey, one of the most notorious of rustlers and a bitter personal enemy. But a certain chivalry rules among such people, and after the greeting of Sterry to Vesey there was little danger of the latter taking unfair advantage of it.

"This is bad business," remarked the younger, pointing to the figure on the ground.

A hard look crossed the face of the rustler and his thin lips compressed as he shook his head.

"Yes, that's what's left of Jack Perkins; he was my pard."

"How did it happen?"

"How did it happen! A pretty question for you to ask. He was killed by the stockmen less than an hour ago."

"But they didn't ride hither and shoot him down, I am sure."

"I don't know what you can be sure of," said Vesey, ominously.

"Jack and I were riding along peaceable like, when we heard horsemen behind us. We didn't pay any attention to them till we got home and Jack slipped off his horse. I concluded to stay in the saddle until the fellows came up and I had a talk with them. They were Capt. Asbury and his stockmen, and the first thing they called out was an order for us to throw up our hands.

"Well," continued Vesey, grimly, "we aren't in that kind of business, and the next thing the guns were popping all around us. Jack had nerve. I wish the poor fellow had stayed in the saddle; but his horse scooted off, and he stood right there where he fell, without a leaf to shelter him, and pumped the lead into those stockmen, who were mean enough to shoot the brave fellow in his tracks without giving him a chance for life."

"You told me they ordered him to surrender before the firing began."

"So they did, that they might shoot him down the easier. I had a hot chase with them, and it was a pretty close call for me; but they didn't keep up the hunt for long. You would think," added Vesey, bitterly, "that they would have been satisfied with dropping poor Jack, without burning down our home; but that is the style of the stockmen."

Here was a representative of each of the factions, or associations, so hostile to each other. The rustler knew Monteith Sterry, and must have felt a consuming resentment toward him. His words and manner indicated, too, that he was not averse to a quarrel. He had fought the stockmen more than once, and, with the memory of the recent collision and the advantages on the other side, he welcomed the chance of a conflict on anything like equal terms.

Monteith did not stand in any personal fear of the famous

rustler, and was fully armed and on the alert. Without seeming to do so, he kept a watch on the man, but he disliked the thought of a personal encounter with him. The scene, the surroundings, and his own nature, revolted, and he resolved to submit to all that it was possible to bear before falling back on the last resort.

"No doubt," said Sterry, "there has been injustice on both sides, and stockmen as well as rustlers have done things for which there is no justification; I hope the trouble will soon end."

"It will end as soon as we get justice."

"Yes," Sterry could not help retorting, "for if justice were done to you rustlers none would be left. However," he hastened to add, "there is no reason why you and I should quarrel, Vesey; I had no share in the death of your friend; and if the case is as you represent it, he was more sinned against than sinning."

"Of course you had no share in that simply because you wasn't here, but you have been concerned in other affairs like this where some of the rustlers have gone down."

"It is quite possible I have," coolly replied Sterry, "inasmuch as when a man is attacked it is his duty to defend himself. I have not yet been convinced that I ought to stand up and allow others to do as they please when weapons were in my hands."

"You have no business in Wyoming anyway," said Vesey, angrily; "you have been sent here by the Association to do its underhand work."

"Duke Vesey," said Sterry, "you are a man of too much

education to talk in that way. If you and I quarrel, it will be your fault, but don't fancy that I hold you in any fear. Good-night."

Edward S. Ellis

CHAPTER XX

THE TRUCE

It was a dignified proceeding on the part of Monteith Sterry, and the rustler possessed enough gentlemanly instinct to appreciate the feelings of the young man, who had attested his courage too often for any one to question it. But at the moment of wheeling his mare to ride off both caught the sound of approaching horsemen, and Sterry checked his animal.

"Who are they?" he asked, glancing at the rustler.

"How should I know? They may be some of your folks."

"They are as likely to be yours. I don't think, Duke, it is wise for us to stay here where we offer such inviting targets, for whoever the party may be, one of us is sure to be an enemy."

Monteith Sterry moved away from the area of illumination as he spoke, Vesey keeping close to his side.

"Is it understood, Duke," asked the younger, "there's a truce between you and me?"

"Of course; if you know anything about Duke Vesey, you

know he's square. If they happen to be some of our boys, I won't take any advantage of you, nor let them, if I can help it."

"And if they are Capt. Asbury and others, I will reciprocate."

Enough was said. Enemies though the men were, no bosom friends could have been more in unison for the time. Ready to shoot each other on sight less than an hour before, and as they were liable to be within the following hour, they were equally ready to risk their lives, if necessary, to carry out the pledge just exchanged.

They had to ride but a short way when the gloom became deep enough to protect them against the sight of the horsemen who were approaching from the opposite direction.

Six men rode into view, halting on the spot vacated by the couple just before, the one at the head being recognized in the glow of the burning ruins as Capt. Asbury, with whom the affray had taken place a short time previous. Sterry knew each, as did his companion.

"All the party do not seem to be there," remarked Sterry.

"They are not," replied Vesey; "three are missing."

"I wonder if anything can have happened to them?"

"Accidents are liable to take place in this part of the world—"

"Hands up!" was the startling command that broke upon the couple at that moment, from a point directly behind them.

The truth was, Sterry and Vesey had been seen by the horsemen as they stole away in the gloom. Capt. Asbury, suspecting they were rustlers, sent three of his men out beyond them on foot, and they did their part so well that they came up without alarming either of their horses, who ordinarily would have detected them.

"I've been trapped!" muttered Vesey, savagely, glancing at the figures, standing but a short way off in the moonlight, with their Winchesters levelled.

"Never mind," said Sterry, quickly, "up with your hands, as I do, or we'll both catch it; I'll stand by you."

The rustler was wise enough to obey, with only a momentary hesitation. Had he not done so, he would never have had a second chance, for the stockmen were very much in earnest.

The footmen came forward with their weapons at a level, for they were too prudent to give their prisoners a chance.

"How are you, Hendricks?" asked Sterry, with a laugh, as the trio joined them.

The man addressed peered closely in his face, suspecting, and yet not convinced of his identity until after a minute or two.

"Well, I'll be hanged!" he exclaimed; "is that you, Mont?"

"I have a suspicion that it is," was the reply of Sterry, laughing quite heartily as he lowered his hands.

"Who is your friend?" he asked, moving around to gain a better view of the rustler.

"Ah, that's the man we're looking for," added Hendricks a moment later; "he's Duke Vesey, the partner of the late Jack Perkins."

"You are right," Sterry hastened to say, "but he is under the protection of a flag of truce."

"A flag of truce!" repeated the other; "where is it?"

"I gave him my pledge to shield him against you folks, as he agreed to do if your party had proven to be his friends."

"Well, that's a queer state of affairs," laughed the other, not forgetting to keep guard of the prisoner, who was permitted to lower his hands. The other stockmen were equally alert, now that there was but one man to watch, so that Vesey was really as helpless as though deprived of all his weapons.

"I do not see what is so queer about it," replied Sterry, warmly; "we heard you coming and moved off out of sight. Before doing so Vesey pledged himself to stand by me against any of his friends, if it became necessary, and I promised to do the same for him. The issue shows that it is my privilege to keep my promise—that's all."

It was plain that Hendricks felt himself in a quandary. He had been sent out to capture the two men under the supposition that they were rustlers. It was proved that one of them was the very individual whom Capt. Asbury was anxious to secure. To release him after taking him prisoner would place his captor in anything but a pleasant situation with his leader.

Suspecting his dilemma, Sterry said:

"You can readily arrange it by taking me in as prisoner and allowing Vesey to go."

"That is all well enough, but it will put me in a hole that I don't intend to be put in. Capt. Asbury is the boss of this business; you two can ride up to him and make your report; that will place the responsibility where it belongs."

This seemed reasonable, but Sterry felt uneasy. He knew the violent temper of Capt. Asbury, and feared he would refuse to acknowledge the agreement as binding upon him. On the other hand, Sterry was determined to stand by his pledge to the last.

"I can't consent to that," he said.

"You've got to," replied Hendricks; "it is idle to suppose that any such bargain as you may choose to make can be binding on others who were not present when it was made, and therefore were not parties to it."

"That is one way of putting it, but the promise is binding on me, and as true as I am a living man I will fight to the death against you and the whole party before this person shall suffer because of his faith in my word."

"Very well, then, fight it is; he has got to surrender to Capt. Asbury and await what he is willing to do with him."

"Duke," said Sterry, turning to the rustler, "it's two of us against three, and you and I have been there before."

But on the verge of the explosion the rustler came to the rescue.

"There's no need of any row, Sterry; I'll surrender and take my chances."

And to settle the dispute he struck his horse into a gallop, and before the surprise was over rode up to the group, who were gazing wonderingly off in the gloom, whence came the sound of voices.

Sterry and the footmen were but a brief space behind them. While the astonished captain and his companions were looking around for an explanation, Mont Sterry made it in as brief and pointed words as were at his command.

Capt. Asbury fixed his gray eyes upon the handsome countenance of the young man during the few minutes he was speaking, and Sterry saw, despite the forceful terms in which he stated the agreement, that the leading stockman was angry.

"I've no objection," he remarked, striving to control his voice, which was tremulous with anger, "if you choose to play the woman, but I don't see what I've got to do with it."

"Vesey surrendered under my promise that he should be protected; had he not believed that promise he would not have surrendered."

"But would have been shot down where he sat in the saddle. Had he been beyond reach and come in under such a pledge, the case would have been altogether different; but as it is—"

The fateful words were interrupted by a rush and dash. Attention had been diverted for the moment from the prisoner to the one who was pleading for him and to him who held his fate in his hands. The observant Vesey saw the inevitable trend of events, and, taking advantage of the chance, was off like a thunderbolt.

The parting glimpse showed him leaning forward on his horse, who was plunging at utmost speed straight away in the gloom. A half dozen shots were sent after him and something like pursuit was attempted, but brief as was the start gained it was sufficient, and he was soon beyond all danger.

CHAPTER XXI

A MESSENGER IN HASTE

The daring escape of the prisoner did not tend to improve the temper of Capt. Asbury, and he indulged in a number of emphatic expressions, during which Monteith Sterry was dignified enough to hold his peace.

But the leader of the stockmen quickly recovered his self-poise and accepted the matter as one of the peculiar incidents liable to take place at any time.

His version of the difficulty with the rustlers differed from that given by Vesey. They rode up to the house, not knowing who dwelt there, and were received with a shot, which, fortunately, did no damage. Duke Vesey was at the rear, near the structure in which the horses were stabled, when he hurriedly mounted and dashed off, just as he had recently done. He did not make a fight like his companion, who, as was represented, stood his ground. He was repeatedly summoned to surrender, but paid no heed to it, and it became a choice whether to shoot him down or allow him to empty the saddles.

While Sterry could not feel so well disposed toward Vesey after hearing this account, he did not regret the part he had acted, and he was also suspicious that Capt. Asbury had tinged his version with a little romance.

The incident itself was of small moment, but the consequences were likely to be far-reaching and important. One of the rustlers had fallen and his companion had escaped. His story of the fight would place the blame wholly upon the stockmen and inflame the feeling between the rustlers and ranchmen, already at a dangerous intensity.

Capt. Asbury was out with his men for the purpose of arresting several of the most notorious of the offenders against the law. Those rustlers were sufficiently powerful to make trouble. If they were given time to organize they could sweep the captain and his little party from the earth. There was reason to believe they would do that very thing, now that Duke Vesey was at liberty to spread his account of the last outrage.

Capt. Asbury held a brief consultation with his men, all, including Sterry, taking part. The consensus of opinion was that they ought to effect a junction with some of the larger parties of stockmen known to be abroad, or withdraw to some safe point like Buffalo, Riverside, or the nearest military station.

Ira Inman, Larch Cadmus and the others were on the "warpath," and at no great distance. Morning would probably find them in sight, if the stockmen should stay where they were.

Capt. Asbury decided to ride to the westward, in the hope of effecting a junction with friends or of reaching a point where they would be secure against their assailants.

The night was well advanced, but their horses had done comparatively little travelling and were capable of a good deal more. The captain took the lead, holding only occasional converse with his men as he swung along at an easy pace; but he, like the rest, was on the lookout for danger, which was liable to approach from any point of the compass.

A marked change showed itself in the temperature. The weather, as will be remembered, had been unusually mild earlier in the evening, but it now became sharp and chilly, as though the breath from the snowy mountain crests was wafted down upon them.

In a valley-like depression, an hour later, where there was an abundance of grass, beside a flowing stream of water, the party went into camp, with a couple of their number on guard, just as they would have done if in a hostile country—which in point of fact was the case.

The night passed, however, without any disturbance, and all were astir before sunrise. The men were provided with several days' rations, while the succulent grass afforded the animals all the food they needed, so there was no trouble on that score.

Capt. Asbury and Monteith Sterry mounted their horses and rode to the crest of the nearest elevation, which was fully 100 feet in height and commanded a wide sweep of country. The morning was clear and bright, and the first glance they cast to the northward revealed a stirring sight. A horseman was less than a half-mile away, and riding at headlong speed, as if in the extremity of mortal fright.

"What can it mean?" asked the puzzled leader; "no one is pursuing him, and I see no cause for his panic."

"I suspect," replied Sterry, thoughtfully, "that he is a messenger bringing important tidings to you."

CHAPTER XXII

IMPORTANT TIDINGS

It seemed strange that the messenger, if such he was, should know the right course to follow in order to reach the camp of Capt. Asbury, for he was riding directly toward it, and that, too, at the highest speed of which his horse was capable.

But Monteith Sterry had noted a fact which escaped the captain, though he was an observant man. The horseman was not approaching the camp at the moment the couple reached the crest of the elevation and began scrutinizing the surrounding country; he was going at right angles to it, but (as it afterward proved) he carried a glass, with which, at that moment, he was also scanning the horizon for something he was very anxious to find.

Fortunately he caught sight of the couple, and though he could not be assured of their identity at so great a distance, the suspicion of the truth as to Capt. Asbury caused him to put his animal to his best speed.

In a brief time he rode up. While some rods away he recognized the captain and saluted him. A little nearer approach and he identified Sterry, who was astonished beyond measure to discover that he was his old friend, Dick

Hawkridge, toward whose ranch he had ridden on the preceding evening.

"You're out early, Dick," was the salutation of Sterry, as his old friend reined up beside him and extended his hand.

"And are riding hard," added Capt. Asbury, who liked the young man.

"I ride hard," replied Hawkridge, gravely, "because there is need of it; I was looking for you."

"And why looking for me?" inquired the captain.

"Because you and your men are in great peril."

"Ah. What might be its nature?"

"From the rustlers."

"I was trying to persuade myself that it was they who were in peril from us, but you put it differently."

"It might be as you wish if you had twenty-five or fifty men; but with less than a dozen, and more than twice that number looking for you, discretion is the better part of valor."

"Tell me, Hawkridge, how all this interesting information came to you," continued Capt. Asbury.

"My ranch is not far to the northward, my cattle are ranging among the foothills of the Big Horn Mountains, and all my hands are with them. I sat up late last night, going over my accounts and trying to get them into shape, and it was past midnight when two rustlers rode up. I supposed they meant to stay all night and invited them in. I have never had any trouble with them, and they had two purposes in calling. One was to give me a little advice, and the other to secure information."

"Their advice, I suppose, was that you cast in your fortunes with them, and take up the business of branding mavericks and altering other brands."

"Hardly that, but it was that I should keep out of the trouble, for there are going to be ugly times. Now you know that, however much I may wish to let things proceed smoothly, I will never identify myself with the law-breakers. I gave my callers to understand that, and I think they respect my position.

"It seems to me," added Hawkridge, thoughtfully, "that there have been some woeful mistakes made. The Cattle Association have organized an expedition to rid Johnson, Natroma and Converse Counties of cattle-thieves, as they call them. They have imported twenty-five picked men from Texas, every one of whom is a fighter and dead shot, with Capt. Smith, an ex-U.S. marshal, as their leader. One of the party may be taken as a type of the rest. He is Scott Davis, once a guard on the Deadwood coach, and he carries a gun with twenty notches on the stock, each representing the death of a road-agent or other outlaw.

"The expedition left Cheyenne some days ago and is somewhere in this section. Strong as it is, it is doomed to defeat, for I don't care how brave and skilful those fellows are, they are no more so than the rustlers, who far outnumber them.

"However, it isn't that which concerns you and me just now, though it may do so later. The rustlers have learned that you are out with a small party, and they are after you."

Capt. Asbury was a brave man, and he did not start on hearing this announcement, for he had been expecting it from the first; but he was prudent as well as daring, and he knew his young friend did not underestimate the danger of himself and companions.

"Have they learned anything about last night's doings?" asked Sterry.

"That's what started me off after you in such a hurry. My callers stayed more than two hours, and were about leaving when who should ride up but Duke Vesey, with his story of the killing of his comrade, Jack Perkins, by you and your men."

"I suppose he called it a murder," remarked Capt. Asbury, sarcastically.

"Yes, the worst kind, too. I knew he was drawing a long bow, but he will tell it to others, and it will spread like wildfire. He was looking for Ira Inman, Larch Cadmus and his party. There are more of them than you and others are aware of, riding up and down the country, ripe for any mischief. From what I know, Inman and a dozen of the most desperate rustlers are in the neighborhood, and as the two fellows who were at my ranch volunteered to help Vesey find them they will do it pretty soon, if they have not already done so. Vesey declared it as his belief that you would be discovered not far from his burned home, so as soon as they left I mounted my best horse and started to give you warning."

"I appreciate your kindness, Hawkridge; how did you know the right direction?"

"I knew the course to Vesey's ranch, and was speeding that

way when I caught sight of you and Sterry on the top of this hill. I took a squint through my glass, was pretty sure who it was, and then came like mad. I didn't suspect it was you though, Mont, until I almost ran against you."

"Did Vesey say anything about me?" asked Sterry, with a meaning glance at the captain.

"He said you had acted like a white man in some dispute, but he didn't give the particulars and I didn't question him. He is intensely bitter against the captain and his party, and declares that not one of them shall get out of the country alive; and, captain, Duke Vesey is a man of his word."

"Then I suppose I may consider myself disposed of," replied Asbury, with a laugh.

"Not as bad as that, but it depends upon yourself."

"What do you advise?"

"Start southward at once with your men; if you meet the Texans and their friends, join them if you choose; it will make their strength so much the greater, and they need it all. If you fail to meet them, keep on till you cross the Platte and strike Fort Fetterman. In other words, captain, you have no business to be where you are."

CHAPTER XXIII

AT BAY

Capt. Asbury drew a cigar from his pocket and lit it, first offering one to each of his companions. He puffed in silence for a minute or two, evidently absorbed in thought. He was a veteran of the civil war, and had learned to be cool in dangerous crises.

"Hawkridge," he remarked, removing his cigar, "you are right in the main, although not wholly so."

"I await correction."

"Doubtless it is all true what you say about the festive rustlers roaming up and down the land seeking whom they may devour, but you forget that, leaving out the quarter of a hundred from the Lone Star State, there are also other bands of stockmen abroad. Now, if we could effect a junction with one or two of those companies, why, you'll admit, the aspect of affairs will be changed."

"Unquestionably; but consider how slight the chance—"

"On the contrary, I think the prospect is good. Now, if you'll be kind enough to level your glass to the eastward, possibly you will observe something interesting."

Both young men quickly turned their heads in the direction indicated, and there, sure enough, was descried a body of horsemen, probably a mile distant, approaching on a gallop.

Hawkridge levelled his glass. While thus engaged, Capt. Asbury signalled to his men to mount and be ready to move on a moment's call.

It was well to be ready for any emergency.

Dick Hawkridge studied the horsemen closely for some minutes without speaking. Then, with his eye still at the glass, he repeated slowly, as if to himself:

"There are thirteen of them, and the spotted horse at the head I am sure belongs to Ira Inman; the whole party are rustlers."

He lowered the binocular and looked at the captain, adding:

"I suspected it; their party is but a little stronger than yours, for Mont and I will stand with you, but it seems to me it would be foolish to risk a fight in the open."

"I am willing to retreat, but I don't intend to be run out of Wyoming by all the rustlers between Sheridan and Cheyenne. I am willing, however," he added, with a smile, "to make a strategical movement to the rear until we strike some place where there's a show for defence; do you know of any such place?"

"My house is well fitted for that, and is not far off."

"All right; lead on."

Edward S. Ellis

By this time the rest of the party had ridden to the top of the hill, where the situation was quickly made clear to them. They looked off at the party of rustlers, and several expressed the wish that the captain would stay and fight them; but he replied that they were quite certain to get enough of fighting before they were many days older, and he followed Hawkridge.

At sight of the flight, the rustlers uttered tantalizing shouts and discharged their Winchesters in the air. At the same time they increased the speed of their animals; but, as they were no better mounted than the stockmen, there was little chance of overtaking them.

The surface was undulating, the ground being well covered with verdure even thus early in the spring. Sometimes pursuers and fugitives were out of sight of each other for a minute or two, but not long enough to affect the situation.

The course was northwest, and Hawkridge was hopeful that they would reach his ranch in an hour or a little more. And this they probably would have done had they not been interrupted, or rather checked, by the unexpected appearance of a third company of horsemen, almost directly in front of the stockmen.

"It may be they are friends," said Capt. Asbury, instantly bringing his horse down to a walk, as did the others.

But the hope was delusive. A brief scrutiny of the strangers through the glass by Dick Hawkridge left no doubt that they, too, were rustlers, probably engaged on the same errand as Inman and his men.

This, of course, overthrew the plan of taking refuge at the ranch of Hawkridge, with a view of defending themselves, for to push on insured a collision with the party in front. They seemed to be about as numerous as Inman's company, and as the latter were sure to arrive before anything could be accomplished by the most spirited attack on the rustlers, it would have been folly to incur such a risk.

The most obvious course was to turn to the left, with no special object except to reach some place that could be used as a means of defence. In a country with such a varied surface it ought not to take long to find a refuge.

Dick Hawkridge, when leading the way to his home, acted as guide, and now that the change was made he continued to do so because of his familiarity with the country. Beside him rode his friend, Mont Sterry, with Capt. Asbury and the rest following in loose order.

It was an interesting question as to how Inman and the others would act upon meeting, and the stockmen watched for the junction.

At the moment the abrupt turn was made in the course of the fugitives the two parties of rustlers did not see each other, a precipitous ridge preventing. They must have been puzzled, therefore, to understand the cause of the sudden change in the line of flight.

The mystery, however, was speedily cleared up, and the rustlers greeted each other with ringing cheers, adding a few derisive shouts to the fleeing stockmen. They were seen to mingle for a short time only, while they discussed the situation. Then the company, increased to more than a score, galloped after the cattlemen.

A fight was inevitable, for the flight and pursuit could not continue indefinitely. Brave and confident, the rustlers were

Edward S. Ellis

ardent for the opportunity, while Capt. Asbury and his men were equally eager to come upon some place which would do something toward equalizing the strength of the combatants.

It was humiliating thus to flee before the very men whom he had set out to arrest, but what veteran has not been obliged to do humiliating things in the course of his career?

"This flight can't continue much longer," quietly remarked Monteith Sterry to Hawkridge, at his side.

"Why not?"

"The men are dissatisfied and are unwilling to keep it up. We have let those fellows approach so near that their bullets come uncomfortably close.

"Capt. Asbury is growing impatient; I shouldn't wonder if he gives the order to stop and have it out with them. It will be warm work if we do, but over that next ridge I think we shall gain sight of a good place for making a stand."

Something in the appearance of the surroundings was familiar to Sterry, but he could not identify them.

Just then two of the rustlers fired their guns, and the pinge of one of the bullets was plainly heard. Sterry looked around and saw Capt. Asbury compress his lips and shake his head; he did not like the way things were going. A crisis was at hand.

The top of the ridge being attained, all saw a large structure below, and not far off.

"Do you recognize it?" asked Hawkridge, with a smile.

"No—why, yes; is it possible?"

"You ought to know it, for, if I am not mistaken, you are considerably interested in one member of the family."

"I never supposed we were so near Fred Whitney's home," was the amazed comment of Sterry, who was in doubt whether, under the circumstances, he ought to be pleased or not.

"There's where we'll make a stand," called out Capt. Asbury, "and let the music begin."

Edward S. Ellis

CHAPTER XXIV

THE PRIMITIVE FORT

"Move a little lively, boys," added the captain, spurring his horse to a faster gait; "there'll be some shooting, and they're closer than they ought to be."

By a providential coincidence, the whole party of rustlers halted before ascending the ridge, which would give them a view of the building in which the stockmen were about to make a stand. They probably saw the impossibility of overtaking the fugitives by a direct pursuit, and paused to decide upon some different course of action.

This was proven by what they did a few minutes later, for they separated into two divisions, one turning to the right and the other to the left. They seemed to think that the course of their enemies must change soon, in which case there was a chance of heading them off and bringing them between two fires. The rustlers were more familiar with the country than the stockmen, and, had the chase continued, it is likely it would have resulted as they expected.

But, strangely enough, these people forgot the Whitney home, upon which it may be said the horsemen stumbled the next moment.

Down the ridge rode the dozen or more, Hawkridge, Sterry and Capt. Asbury at the head, with the others almost upon their heels. In the brisk morning air the frightened Jennie Whitney hastened to the door and gazed wonderingly upon the party.

She recognized the handsome youth, who doffed his hat, a courtesy instantly imitated by Hawkridge, the captain, and then the rest of the men, as they halted in front of the door, where stood the pale and startled mother, at a loss to understand the meaning of the strange sight.

"Good-morning!" called Sterry. "Where's Fred?"

"He's on the range with the men, looking after the cattle."

"And are you and your mother alone?"

"We are the only ones in the house. What is the meaning of all this?" she asked, looking with astonishment at the horsemen.

"We are pursued by a company of rustlers," replied Hawkridge; "they are directly behind us; I started to lead our friends to my ranch, but they headed us off, and we were compelled to apply here for shelter."

"You are welcome," Mrs. Whitney hastened to say; "dismount and come in as soon as you can."

Sterry, Hawkridge and Capt. Asbury thanked her simultaneously. Time was beyond value. They expected every instant to hear the crack of the rifles and the shouts of their enemies on the crest of the ridge, and could not comprehend why they were delayed.

They dashed to the structure at the rear and a short distance from the dwelling, into which they ran their horses, slipped off their trappings, and hurried back to the house.

Every one was inside and not a shot fired, nor was a rustler seen. It was beyond explanation.

But the stockmen were wise enough to turn to the best account the grace thus given to them.

They stationed themselves at the front and rear doors and windows with loaded weapons, on the alert to wing the first rustler who showed himself.

Sterry found time to exchange a few words with Jennie and her mother.

"It is too bad," he said, "to put you to this trouble and danger; but the rustlers outnumber us more than two to one, and it was the only hope that offered itself."

"And glad am I that it *did* present itself. O, if my poor husband had been here when they attacked him!"

"When do you expect the return of Fred?"

"Not before night, and the hands may not come with him. He does not dream of anything like this."

"Nor did we, a little while ago. Had any other refuge presented itself we would have seized it; but I never suspected we were near your home until we came over the ridge and saw it but a few rods away."

"But, where are they?" asked the wondering Jennie.

"That's something I don't understand, for they were near enough for their bullets to whistle about our ears."

"They have seen where you took shelter and are afraid to attack you."

"That may be; but why don't they show themselves?"

At this moment Capt. Asbury approached. Repeating his regrets that they should place their friends in such danger, he said:

"As there is no saying how long we shall have to stay here, we ought to learn the nature of our defences. Our horses are in the stables, where, if the rustlers choose, they can get them, and they will be pretty sure to choose to do it. They can steal to the rear of the sheds and take them out without risk. Now, Mrs. Whitney, we have enough rations with us to last, in a pinch, for three or four days; how are you fixed?"

"We have but a small quantity of food in the house—none worth mentioning."

"No matter how slight, it is worth mentioning. Under the circumstances, I think we can say we are provisioned for the whole time of the siege, which must be over in less than a week."

"But how will it end?" asked the lady.

The captain shrugged his shoulders.

"Take no thought of the morrow; but what worries me is the question of water—how about that?"

A hurried examination disclosed that there was not quite two pailfuls in the house. Even that was more than usual. The small stream from which the supply was obtained was beyond the stables in which the horses were sheltered. Water from that source was out of the question while the siege continued.

Several of the men had a small quantity in their canteens, but, inasmuch as no such contingency as this was antici-pated, little preparation had been made.

Still Capt. Asbury expressed himself gratified at the result of his investigation. The weather was so cool that a moderate amount of the precious fluid would prevent suffering, and he decided that, dispensing with what ordinarily was used for cooking purposes, they could get along quite well for three days, and possibly longer.

The lower part of the flat building consisted of two parts, used respectively for the kitchen and the dining and sitting-room. There were four apartments above—one for the parents, one each for the son and daughter, and one for visitors. These, of course, would be held sacred for the members of the family, while the others found sleep, as opportunity presented, below stairs.

There were windows on all sides of the house; and the structure, while not strong, was, of course, bullet-proof.

Before all this was ascertained the rustlers showed them-selves. But instead of appearing on the ridge, over which the cattlemen had ridden, half of them showed themselves on the other side, having circled around back of the stables.

A moment later the rest were observed on top of the ridge. Thus, with the exception of the broad level plain stretching in the direction of the Big Horn Mountains, it may be said that the ranch was surrounded by the rustlers, who held the stockmen at bay.

What would be the result? None could foresee.

Hawkridge drew Sterry aside and said, in a guarded undertone:

"There is only one thing to be feared."

"What is that?"

"It is easy for them to burn this building."

"Do you think they will do that, when they know a couple of women are inside?"

"It doesn't follow that there is any necessity of their being burned, nor indeed of any of us suffering from fire. When you touch off a barn the rats get out, and that's what we shall have to do."

"But they will give us a chance, first."

"Yes, a chance to surrender, and we might have done that without putting ourselves to all this trouble."

"And suppose we *do* surrender, after making the best fight we can—what are likely to be the terms offered?"

"They will treat the majority, including myself, as prisoners of war; but Capt. Asbury, and probably you, will be excepted—he because of the killing of Perkins last night, and you because you have disregarded the warning to leave the country when ordered to do so."

"All of which is mighty interesting to the captain and myself," remarked Sterry, with little evidence of fear; "but we will hope for better things."

CHAPTER XXV

THE FLAG OF TRUCE

In one important respect the combatants showed commendable discretion. Although there had been considerable firing on the part of the rustlers, none of the cattlemen were hurt. It is not unlikely that the bullets were intended to frighten them, since such excellent marksmen otherwise could not have discharged their weapons without execution.

Capt. Asbury and his men had not returned a shot. When their enemies appeared on more than one side of the building it would have been easy to pick off several without risk to those sheltered within the house, but he gave orders that nothing of that sort should be done.

The bitterness between the parties was already intense. There were hot-heads on both sides eager to open the lamentable conflict, but were it done, there was no saying where it would end. It was wise, therefore, that the leaders forbore from active hostilities at this early stage of the business.

From the front of the structure the plain stretched in the direction of the Big Horn Mountains. It was across this that Jennie Whitney descried, two days before, the return of her friends with the body of her father. She now ascended to the second story and peered long and frequently in the same direction, in the hope of catching sight of her brother.

Meanwhile Capt. Asbury disposed of the members of his party as best he could. They needed no instructions from him to avoid in every way possible annoying the ladies, who were considerate and kind.

About midday, excitement was caused among the besieged by the appearance of a flag of truce. A man rode over the ridge, down which the cattlemen had come in such haste, holding a white handkerchief fluttering over his head. His horse walked slowly and the rider kept his gaze on the front of the house, as though in doubt of the reception awaiting him. A hundred feet away he came to a halt, still flourishing the peace signal above his hat.

Capt. Asbury was the first to discover the messenger and hurriedly arranged for the interview.

"Inasmuch as that fellow is neither Inman, Cadmus, nor anyone of the leaders, it is not the thing for me to meet him."

"You have recognized him?" was the inquiring remark of Hawkridge, glancing with a smile at the officer.

"No. Who is he?"

"Duke Vesey, who does not feel particularly amiable toward you."

"I will meet him," volunteered Monteith Sterry. The captain shook his head.

"While that fellow is friendly to you, perhaps, others of the company are very resentful; it isn't best to tempt them.

Hawkridge, you are the best one to act."

"Very well; I will do so."

The horseman had come to a stop and was gazing fixedly at the building, as if waiting for a response to his advance.

Jennie Whitney descended the stairs at this moment.

"I think I see Fred coming," she said, with some agitation; "will they do him any harm?"

"No," replied Sterry, "they have nothing against him."

"But the other day—" she ventured, doubtfully.

"Was a scrimmage, likely to take place at any time; that is ended, but they will probably hold him prisoner."

During this brief conversation a brisk search was going on among the three men for a white pocket-handkerchief. None of them possessed such an article, the hue in each case being different. Hawkridge appealed to Miss Whitney, and she produced a linen handkerchief of snowy whiteness.

"Just the thing," he said, drawing back the door sufficiently to allow him to pass out. "I don't think I will be detained long. It is understood," he added, turning to the captain, "that we don't consider the question of surrender under any terms."

"It will be better to report, and then decide what to do."

Hawkridge bowed and passed out. He waved the spotless linen in front of his face as he walked toward the horseman, and both smiled when they recognized each other.

"Well, Duke, what is it?" asked the footman, as though he were asking an ordinary question of a friend.

"I reckon you can guess. Since the two companies came together Ira Inman is at the head of the army. Some of the boys are wild to begin shooting, and they'll do it pretty soon. Before that, Inman decided to offer you folks a chance to give in. That's my business."

"You simply demand our surrender, as I understand it?"

"You've guessed it the first time," replied Vesey, with a nod of his head.

"What terms do you offer?"

"You'll be treated as prisoners of war; but," added the rustler, "it is hardly right to say that. It's Inman's idea to hold you as hostages for the right treatment of any of our boys that may fall into the hands of the stockmen."

"That is quite different. Let me ask, Duke, whether this treatment is guaranteed to all of our folks?"

"I wish I could say it was, Dick, but I can't; Inman makes two exceptions—Capt. Asbury and Mont Sterry. That Sterry showed himself so much of a man and was so square toward me when I was caught that I would do anything I could for him. I appealed to Inman to let up on him, but he won't; some of the boys are so mad they will shoot him on sight."

"And Capt. Asbury?"

Vesey's face became hard.

"He ought to be hanged because of the way he acted

last night."

"But what is proposed to do with him and Sterry?"

"Give them a fair trial."

Hawkridge shook his head with a meaning smile.

"It won't work, Duke; there isn't a man in our company who would consent to anything of the kind. There could be but one issue to such a trial, and it would be nothing less than the betrayal of our leader or a comrade by us."

"Inman declares he will burn down the house if you refuse his terms."

"Let him try it as soon as he pleases; you can tell him for Capt. Asbury that his terms are rejected."

Edward S. Ellis

CHAPTER XXVI

THE UNDERGROUND MISSIVE

Dick Hawkridge, standing on the ground, looked up in the bronzed face of Duke Vesey, sitting in the saddle.

At every window on the lower floor were faces watching the two men that had thus met under a flag of truce. From the ridge on the right, and the undulating ground to the left, peered the rustlers, intensely interested in the actions of the couple, whose words were spoken in tones too low to reach the ears of any on either side. No actors ever had a more attentive audience than they.

When Hawkridge announced to Vesey that his proffer was rejected (for it was useless to report first to Capt. Asbury, as he had been told to do), the horseman said:

"Dick, you would have been a cur to accept such terms, though I would do anything to even matters with that Asbury; but I want to get a message to Mont Sterry."

"You can trust me to carry it."

"It is for him alone; I have it in writing. Well, good-by."

He leaned over from the saddle and extended his hand. As Hawkridge took it he felt something in his palm.

"I understand," he said; "it shall be delivered."

No one watching the couple, as nearly all were doing, suspected this little by-play. They saluted, and Vesey spurred his pony to a gallop, passing up the ridge and joining his friends to report, while Hawkridge was admitted through the door, which was immediately closed and secured behind him.

To the captain and the others who crowded around he quickly told what had passed.

"Your order was to let you know the terms before giving an answer," he added, addressing the leader, "but you see it wasn't necessary."

A buzz of commendation left no doubt of the wisdom of his course.

"But what about his threat to burn the building?" asked Sterry, addressing no one in particular.

"He will do it, or at least will try it," replied Hawkridge, "for he doesn't intend any one shall have time to interfere, as may be the case if he delays too long."

"To set fire to the house," remarked the captain, who had given much thought to the question, "they must first reach it, and that manoeuvre will prove a costly one to them. I suspect that some other firing will take place about that time—eh, boys?"

The response revealed the feelings of the men, who were

chafing under their restraint.

"But, surely," continued Sterry, "they do not mean to burn the building while Mrs. Whitney and her daughter are within?"

"As was said some time ago," replied Hawkridge, "that makes little difference, since it is not to be supposed that even we will stay inside during the conflagration. The firing is meant to drive us out, and it will do it."

"But there must be considerable shooting, and the ladies will be in danger."

"I think Inman will order us to send them out, so as to prevent harm to them."

"If they were Sioux or Crows they might launch burning arrows and fire-balls; but they can't do that, and will have to run some risk in getting the flames under way."

"There are signs of a storm, and if the night proves dark it will be much in their favor and against us."

"Suppose they fire the stables," suggested one of the men.

"They are too far off to place us in danger, unless a strong wind should blow directly this way."

"Well, boys," said Capt. Asbury, hopefully, "the thing isn't through yet. I think Inman will give us another message before opening the ball, so you may rest easy until he makes his next move."

Meanwhile Hawkridge had managed to deliver the little twist of paper, placed in his hand by Vesey. Inasmuch as the matter had been managed with so much care, he deemed it right that no one should see the transfer to his friend.

Sterry was surprised and glanced down at the object, but, quick to catch on, closed his palm again and took part in the conversation. It was some minutes before he gained a chance to examine the contents unobserved. When he did so, they proved so important that he called Hawkridge and the captain aside and showed the letter to them. Each read it in turn, the contents being as follows:

"FRIEND STERRY: You acted square with me, and I will do the same with you. Inman doesn't expect you folks to accept his terms, for if you do it will be good-by to yourself and Capt. Asbury. It would suit me very well to see him go, as he will if we get a chance at him, but I can't bear the idea of anything bad happening to you after the way you stood by me last night when that Asbury meant to shoot me.

"So my advice is this: Get out of where you are and leave as fast as you know how. Queer advice, you'll think, but I'll show you how you can follow it. A friend of mine, whom we can both trust, and I, will be on watch to-night at the stables. It looks as if it is going to be as dark as a wolf's mouth.

"It won't do to move before 10 o'clock. When everything is ready I will light a cigarette and flirt the match around my head once, as if to put it out. That will mean that the way is open. Steal out of the back door and dodge to the stables; your mare will be ready, and when another chance opens you can make a break. No one can overtake you, and I don't think it will be suspected who you are.

"If you succeed, I hope you will have sense enough to

stay out of Wyoming, at least until this flurry is over. If you are detected while trying to reach the stables you can dart back, for I don't think anyone will shoot at you, since we have orders not to do that until after you folks begin the rumpus.

"Inman means to set fire to the house to-night. He won't be able to hold back the boys much longer. When ready, he will send word and ask the two ladies to come out to him, where he will hold them beyond reach of fire and bullet. He expects there will be the hottest kind of shooting, and it will be a bad thing for you folks. Capt. Asbury may as well make his will, for I'm not the only one that will lay for him.

"Don't forget my directions. It will not be before 10 o'clock, and may be a little later. Don't let any one see this, and don't drop a hint to Asbury. It is meant for your good, and you will act like a sensible man.

"D.V."

CHAPTER XXVII

ON PAROLE

A new matter of interest claimed the immediate attention of the defenders within the home of ranchman Whitney.

It will be remembered that the sister had reported the approach of a horseman, whom she believed to be her brother. The rider was now in plain sight, and a brief scrutiny through the glass by Hawkridge removed all doubt; she was right.

He was coming at an easy, swinging gallop, straight toward his home. He must have seen the rustlers while yet a considerable way off, for he quickened the pace of his animal, stirred by a natural anxiety for his loved ones and by a curiosity to know the meaning of the strange condition of affairs.

Had he understood matters fully, while yet at a distance, he would have avoided a mistake which occasioned him and his friends intense regret, and which proved irreparable.

He did not cease his advance until within a hundred yards, when the cattlemen, who were watching his every movement, saw him bring his horse to a sudden halt. At the same moment a couple of rustlers moved into view, their guns held so as to cover him. He sat motionless until they came up, one on either side, when he was seen to be conversing earnestly with them.

"They have made him prisoner," remarked Hawkridge, "just as I was sure they would."

"Will they do him harm?" asked Mrs. Whitney, who, with Jennie, had descended the stairs and stood with the group near the front door.

"No," was Hawkridge's reassuring reply; "he must see the uselessness of resistance, and we are not fighting Indians who learned warfare from the late lamented Sitting Bull."

It was noticed that Fred Whitney, despite the wound of a couple of days before, no longer wore his arm in a sling. As he had said, he was ashamed to do so.

Brave as was the young man, he had judgment. He knew that he was at the mercy of a score of rustlers, and quickly learned the situation. Capt. Asbury, Monteith Sterry, Dick Hawkridge and a number of cattlemen were besieged in his home.

While he was holding earnest converse with his captors one of them turned and addressed Inman, who was out of sight of the besieged, because of the intervening ridge. His reply caused Whitney to dismount and walk in that direction, he, too, passing out of the field of vision.

He was invisible for perhaps ten minutes, when he was seen coming over the ridge toward his own door, but without his Winchester or revolvers. A moment later he was admitted. He kissed his mother and sister and grasped the hands of his friends, who crowded around to congratulate him and hear what he had to say.

"They told me everything," he replied, looking into the glowing faces, and smiling at the anxiety depicted on several. "I have made a woeful mistake, boys."

"How's that?" asked several in the same breath.

"Hankinson and Weber have moved several miles further into the mountains, so nothing will be seen of them for several days, and perhaps not for a week. The trouble with the rustlers makes it necessary that we should keep closer watch than usual upon the stock, and it is understood that they are not to leave the cattle until they get word from me. So, as I said, they are out of the question."

"Is that the mistake you refer to?" asked Sterry.

"I wish it was; but a couple of hours ago, Hankinson, who had ridden a considerable distance beyond the grazing grounds, came in with the report that a large body of men were camped in a valley a mile or so further on. There must be fifty at least."

Capt. Asbury emitted a low whistle.

"Rustlers again! By and by we'll have all there are in Wyoming swarming about this house."

"No; Budd visited them, and found they were cattlemen on the hunt for rustlers. Had he known of Inman's party out here he would have given them a pointer, but of course he doesn't dream of anything of the kind. Now, the mistake I made is this: When I saw the horsemen gathered about the buildings and ridge, I ought to have wheeled and ridden as hard as I could to the stockmen. They would have been here before night and wound up this business in a jiffy. But I kept on and rode right into the trap set for me, and can do nothing."

No one could question the justice of Whitney's self-condemnation, but there was no help for it.

"How is it you were allowed to join us?" asked Capt. Asbury.

"I am here under parole; you see they took my horse, rifle and pistols from me. I would not have been allowed to come to you except upon my pledge to return within fifteen minutes."

"And what will they do with you, my boy?" asked his mother, alarmed by the information.

"Nothing, so long as I remain a model prisoner; but how are you fixed for defence?"

He was quickly made acquainted with the situation of affairs.

"Ah," he added, with a sigh, "if there was some way of getting word to the stockmen; but I see none."

"They will not be likely to give you a chance?"

Fred shook his head.

"I'm afraid I overdid the thing. I asked them to be allowed to go back to my cattlemen, but they would not listen to it. They acted as if they were suspicious, and told me I must stay with them until the trouble ended, which they assured me would be soon."

Sterry glanced significantly at Asbury and Hawkridge. He recalled that singular message from Duke Vesey. If all went well, it might contain a shadow of hope. It was deemed best, however, to make no reference to it, even for the benefit of Whitney, who was questioned until he described as exactly as he could the location of the cattlemen.

The grace had expired. No one thought of advising Whitney to disregard his parole, and no urging could have induced him to do it. He affectionately kissed and embraced mother and sister, warmly shook the hands of his friends again, assured them of his hope that all would come out right, and then, passing through the door, was seen to walk up the ridge and pass over the summit, to take his place among his captors, there to await their pleasure.

"Sterry," said Asbury, drawing him and Hawkridge aside, "you were saying awhile ago that nothing could induce you to accept the offer of Vesey to slip out in the darkness of the night."

"No; as he presented it, such a flight would have been a piece of cowardice altogether different from my flight last night. It would have weakened your defensive force and helped no one but me."

"Now, however, it wears a different aspect."

"Yes, it looks providential, and promises to open the way for the escape of all. I hardly think," added Sterry, with a smile, "that with all of Vesey's gratitude to me he would do what he intends if he foresaw the probable consequences, for it means nothing less than the overthrow of Inman's plans."

"And the baffling of his charitable intentions concerning myself," grimly added the captain.

"It seems to me we forgot one phase of the business," remarked Hawkridge, "and that is the fact that the chances of failure are a hundredfold greater than those of success."

His companions looked questioningly at him.

"Perhaps it will not be difficult for Vesey to secure the placing of himself and friend at the stables, as he promises to do, but it seems unlikely that, with a dark night and the temptation for some of us to try to get away, they will be the only couple that will be on the lookout at that time. But, supposing they are," added Hawkridge, "Sterry will have to mount his horse and ride off. There will be some of the rustlers beyond him, and how can he pass them unchallenged?"

"If it proves too risky to try on horseback I can do it on foot," replied Sterry; "in the darkness I will be taken for one of them, and, if questioned, can throw them off their guard. The tramp to where the stockmen are in camp I judge to be little if any more than five miles, and it won't take me long to travel that after getting clear of these people."

"I have a strong belief that the whole scheme is doomed to failure," said Hawkridge, and Capt. Asbury agreed with him.

CHAPTER XXVIII

THE FINAL SUMMONS

Now came hours of wearisome waiting, especially to the besieged, who found in their close quarters little freedom of movement. Some of the men stretched out on the lower floor and slept; others talked and engaged in games of chance, while a desultory watch was maintained, through the doors and windows, upon the rustlers, several of whom were continually in sight.

Before the afternoon had half passed all doubt of the coming darkness was removed. The sky became heavily clouded, the air was raw and chilly, and no moon was visible.

Several distant rifle-shots were heard an hour later, but no one could conjecture or discover the explanation. Probably they signified nothing.

Fred Whitney showed himself on top of the ridge once, and waved his hand in salutation to his friends. This was done to reassure his mother and sister, who were anxious, despite what he had said to them.

Many longing glances were cast across the broad plain in the direction of the mountains. Like shipwrecked mariners

Edward S. Ellis

scanning the horizon for the rescuing sail, the besieged were hopeful that some good fortune would bring the strong body of stockmen that way; but the vision was rewarded by no such welcome sight.

Capt. Asbury received a shock just before night closed in. So many hours had passed without the exchange of a shot that both parties exposed themselves freely. Had they chosen, a good many might have been picked off; but the general understanding that the hour had not yet come for action, threatened, at times, to change the impending tragedy into a most ordinary situation.

Capt. Asbury was sitting by one of the front windows, smoking his briarwood, and looking nowhere in particular, when he saw a man kneeling on top of the ridge and carefully sighting his gun at him. Before the fellow could secure an aim the officer moved quickly back out of sight, and he vanished.

"I have no doubt it was Duke Vesey," he thought; "what a pity I did not shoot him last night."

He judged it not worth while to tell any of the rest of the incident, but he took care not to tempt the fellow again by a second exposure to his aim.

But for this prompt action on the part of the leader, a frightful conflict must have been precipitated. The shooting of the captain would cause retaliation on the part of the stockmen, and it would instantly become a question as to which could do the most execution.

The occurrence was startling enough of itself, but Capt. Asbury quickly recovered, only to find himself troubled by another matter, which was more serious.

It was the doubt whether the intended crime of Vesey was solely of his own responsibility. Was it not likely that he had received permission from Inman to end the suspense by shooting the captain of the stockmen? The captain knew that he was as much detested by the leading rustlers as by Vesey. Probably the men were growing too impatient to be restrained much longer.

The suspicion appeared more reasonable from the fact that, the leader once "removed," there would remain but the single exception to those guaranteed honorable treatment. Surrender, therefore, would be more probable.

No single shot could do so much to aid the rustlers as that which came near being made.

"This strained situation can't last much longer; I believe it will be settled before the rise of to-morrow's sun."

Monteith Sterry secured more than one chance of a few words with Jennie. The sense of danger naturally draws persons closer together, though the incentive was hardly needed in their case.

"Monteith," said she, as they sat apart by themselves, with the shadow of the coming night gradually closing around, "what is to be the end of all this?"

"I will tell you what I think," he replied, and thereupon read in a guarded voice the letter received from Duke Vesey, after which they burned it, that it might not fall into hands that could injure the sender.

"You can see that we are going to be favoured with a very dark night, and Vesey is so anxious to befriend me that I am sure he will find the way, though Hawkridge and the captain are less confident."

"But suppose they recognize you?"

"They can't do that in the darkness, and my rustling friend will not draw me into a peril that is greater than that of staying here."

"I feel as do Mr. Hawkridge and Capt. Asbury," she said, unable to share his ardour.

"Then do you wish me to stay here?"

"I think it is safer."

"And go up in flame and smoke?"

"Won't you be willing to share the risk with me?" she asked, entering into his half-jocose vein.

"But the rustlers will save you that risk; they will give you a good point of observation, from which you can have a fine view of the scene."

"Suppose mother and I refuse to leave?"

"I am certain you will not do that," said Sterry, gravely, "for you will be in great danger under any circumstances."

"But if we remain they may not try to fire the house."

He shook his head.

"Dismiss all idea of that; do not fancy, because hours have passed without the exchange of a shot, that there is any friendship between the parties. By and by a gun will be fired;

somebody will be hurt, and then they will be at it like so many tigers. No, Jennie," he added, "when the warning comes for you and your mother to withdraw you must do so, not only for your own sake, but for ours."

"And how yours?"

"We—that is, the men—can fight much better when your presence causes them no anxiety."

"But, tell me, do not Capt. Asbury and the rest feel hopeful of beating off the rustlers?"

"Of course they will make a brave fight, and there is a chance of their success, but I shudder when I think of what the cost will be to both sides. How much better if all this can be averted."

"True, indeed! And if I could be assured that you would succeed in reaching the camp of the cattlemen, I would bid you Godspeed."

"I certainly will never reach it by staying here, and I think if my chances were doubly less they ought to be taken for the sake of the good that will come to all."

At this juncture, Capt. Asbury, sitting near the window, called out:

"Here's a visitor!"

In the gloom he was not clearly visible, even though he was seen to advance, and heard to knock on the door. But when the latter was opened, Fred Whitney stepped inside.

Here the gathering darkness was more pronounced, for it was

Edward S. Ellis

not deemed prudent to have a light.

"Inman has sent me with his ultimatum," said the messenger; "he says he has given you abundant time to think over the matter, and wants your decision."

"What are his terms?" asked Capt. Asbury.

"The same as before."

"He promises to treat all of us as prisoners of war, with the exception of Sterry and myself. We are guaranteed a trial, which is another way of saying we shall be shot. I will allow my men to vote on the question," added the leader.

The indignant protests, however, compelled the officer to recall his harsh remark.

"Of course I knew that would be your reply," Fred hastened to say; "and it is what Inman and Cadmus expect. I have been sent to bring my mother and sister out of the house, for the rustlers intend to attack you before morning. That means, too, that they intend to burn it."

The three defenders who were in the secret saw the danger in which this placed Sterry's intended flight.

If the attack were made before 10 o'clock, there could be no possible opportunity for his getting away. Some means, therefore, must be found for deferring the assault until after that hour, if it could be accomplished without arousing the suspicions of the rustlers.

CHAPTER XXIX

A STRANGE OCCURRENCE

"Do you know," inquired Sterry, "how soon it is contemplated making the attack?"

"I have not heard Inman or Cadmus say, but from the talk of the men I judge it will be quite soon."

"Probably within a couple of hours?" "Sooner than that—by 9 o'clock at the latest."

It was the mother who now spoke: "Suppose Jennie and I decline to leave the house?"

"That has been considered," replied the son, "and I am sorry to say it will make no difference. The rustlers are in an uglier mood than before—wrathful because they have been kept idle so long. They can claim that they have given you ample notice, and if you refuse to come out they cannot be held blamable for the consequences."

This would never do, and Hawkridge interposed:

"If the attack cannot be prevented, Fred, it must be delayed."

Edward S. Ellis

"On what grounds?"

"Any that you can think of; they must not disturb us until near midnight."

"But I shall have to give a reason; I am as anxious as you to do my utmost, but I do not see how I can do anything."

The quick wit of Jennie came to the rescue.

"Tell Capt. Inman and Larch Cadmus for me that we have a number of articles we wish to save from destruction; ask them in the name of mother and myself to give us time in which to gather them together."

Fred was silent for a moment.

"At least it will do no harm to try it, even though I do not believe it will be of any use."

"Ask them to make it between 11 and 12; we will then have time to collect all we want—in fact a good deal more time than is necessary."

"I do not see the need of this," replied the brother, who, it need not be repeated, had no knowledge of what was in the minds of the few; "I think I can say that if I do not return in the course of ten or fifteen minutes, you may consider your prayer granted."

Bidding them good-by once more, he passed out of the door and disappeared in the darkness, which had now fully descended and shut from sight the impatient rustlers.

It was a peculiar situation in which the defenders, including the mother and sister, dreaded the return of the head of the household, but the front of the dwelling was watched with an intensity of interest it would be hard to describe.

"By gracious! there he is!" exclaimed Dick Hawkridge, hardly ten minutes after Fred's departure; "it's no use."

A shadowy figure was observed moving across the dark space in front, but while they were waiting for him to enter the door, which was unfastened to admit him, he passed on and vanished in the gloom without checking his motion or speaking.

"That wasn't Fred," whispered Jennie; "I know his walk too well."

"It makes no difference," replied Sterry, "you can depend that he will soon put in an appearance."

But the slow minutes dragged along and nothing was seen of him. By and by a faint hope began to form that the urgent request of the ladies had been conceded, for they insisted that they could see no reason why it should not be.

A full hour passed, and, when it was after 9 o'clock, all doubt was removed. The attack would not be made until close upon midnight. Monteith Sterry would be given the chance, provided Duke Vesey showed the way for him.

The crisis was so near that it was deemed best to let all know what was in contemplation. Capt. Asbury, therefore, explained it to the men, as the daughter had explained to the mother.

"Those fellows can't be trusted," the leader added; "they may seek to give the impression that the delay has been granted, while preparing to assail us when least expected. The night is dark, as you see, and favourable to their plans. Keep the closest watch possible on all sides of the house, for to set fire to it they must approach near enough to touch the building."

"Suppose we catch sight of some one stealing up?" asked one of the cattlemen.

"Challenge him, and if he does not give a satisfactory response, fire."

"What will be a satisfactory response?"

"The voice of Fred Whitney, and I may say of Duke Vesey, or the announcement that the individual is the bearer of a message for us. In the latter case, of course, he will approach from the front. When you shoot, too, boys, you mustn't throw away any shots, for this isn't going to be child's play."

"We understand that," was the significant response of a couple of the stockmen.

It was now growing so late that Sterry placed himself near the rear door to watch for the expected signal from Vesey, feeling, as the minutes passed, a nervousness greater than at any time before.

Since no light burned in the house, the only means of determining the hour was by striking a match and holding it in front of a watch. Hope became high when 10 o'clock was at hand.

Sterry half expected, in case everything promised well, that Vesey would manage to give something in the nature of a preliminary signal, but the closest scrutiny showed nothing of the kind.

Capt. Asbury, who maintained his place near one of the front windows, close to the door, suddenly called:

"Come here a moment, Sterry."

The young man stepped hastily across the room.

"You have everything clear in your mind?" was the question which struck the young man as slightly inopportune.

"Yes; as clear as I can have; why do you ask?"

"I wanted to be certain, for your task is a delicate one; we will hold the door ajar a little while after you go, so that if anything happens, such as their recognizing you, you will be able to dash back. You know it won't do for you to be identified."

"I understand," replied Sterry, who felt that he ought to be at his post.

He hastily stepped back, and as he did so was surprised to find the door drawn open several inches.

"What does that mean?" he asked of the several gathered around in the darkness, whose faces he could not see.

"Why," replied Hawkridge, "what does it mean, indeed? I thought you passed out just now."

"You see I did not. Why do you make such a remark?"

"Some one went out," was the amazing declaration.

Edward S. Ellis

CHAPTER XXX

THE MISSING ONE

Monteith Sterry was astounded by the declaration of Dick Hawkridge that some one had passed through the rear door while he was talking with Capt. Asbury.

"Who was it?" demanded he.

"I told you we thought it was you," replied his friend.

"But you know it wasn't," he replied, impatiently.

"Then I have no idea who it was."

"Some one has taken advantage of the moment I spent with the captain—I wonder if he had anything to do with it," he added, growing unjustly suspicious in his resentment.

He strode across the room; and, knowing where the leader was, demanded:

"What is the meaning of this, Capt. Asbury?"

"The meaning of what?"

"While I was talking a few seconds with you some person slipped out of the back door; do you know anything of it?"

"It is beyond my comprehension," replied the leader in a voice which removed all distrust of him.

And forgetful, in his excitement, of his duty at the front, he stepped hastily to the rear, where most of the men had crowded, despite the orders for them to maintain a strict watch.

"I heard you and the captain speaking," said Hawkridge, in explanation, "but your voices were so low that I would not have identified them anywhere. Supposing you to be where you really were, I stepped to the rear window here and peered out in the gloom where I knew the stable to be—"

"Did you see anything?" interrupted Sterry.

"Not a sign of the signal. While I was straining my eyes to pierce the darkness the door was drawn inward slightly, and a figure moved quickly across the space toward the stables."

"You could not identify it?"

"Of course not, for you see how dark it is, and there was no light; in fact, I hardly saw it before it vanished."

"It is as I supposed," added Sterry, angrily. "Some one fancied he had a better chance by slipping off than in remaining here, and has looked after his own safety. I wish I knew who it was."

"We can soon find out," remarked Capt. Asbury; "our men are not too numerous for me to forget their names and voices."

Edward S. Ellis

He raised his tones and summoned them.

"I don't believe they will attempt to fire the house as long as the ladies are with us," he exclaimed; "some one of our party has been cowardly enough to sneak off. As I call your names, answer."

He proved the truth of what he said. He had eight companions, not counting Hawkridge and Sterry. With little hesitation, for his memory was instantly prompted by others, he pronounced each name, and to every one came the prompt, unmistakable response of the owner.

"One of those rustlers has managed to get in here undiscovered," was the next theory of Sterry, whose temper did not improve at the unaccountable turn of affairs. "I don't see why Inman and the rest delay their attack, when we are only children in their hands; they can do with us as they please—"

All started, for at that moment a sharp rap sounded on the door. Before opening it, Capt. Asbury called out:

"Who's there?"

"It is I—Fred Whitney—let me in, quick!"

He was admitted without an instant's delay, while all crowded around in the darkness.

"Well, you can imagine what I have come for. I made known the request of mother and Jennie, but Inman and Cadmus would not think of granting it at first. I told Cadmus that it was your special request, Jennie, adding a little ornamentation of my own, such as that you knew that when he learned how much it could please you, he could not refuse. I hope I did right, did I not, sister?"

In the slight laugh which followed this question, the reply of the young lady was not heard, and her brother continued:

"Well, I put it so strong that Cadmus fell in with me and persuaded Inman to do the same. They agreed to wait until 10 o'clock, but no longer; so you see I did not accomplish all that I hoped, but it was better than nothing. If I am not mistaken it is past 10 now."

"Not more than a few minutes."

"Well, at any rate, the time is up, and they have sent me to notify you that they will wait no longer. I suppose that you, mother and Jennie, have got together all that you can take away. As I have to escort you back, I will carry the things, unless you smuggle in some of the bedsteads."

"Then it is the intention to attack as soon as the ladies are fairly out of the way?" was the inquiring remark of Capt. Asbury.

"You may depend that it won't be delayed ten minutes."

"Do you know whether they will begin by shooting or trying to set fire to the building?"

"They haven't given me their confidence, but I don't see why they should expect to accomplish as much with their guns as they could have done during the day time. They will set fire to the place, no doubt."

"It may be well to impress upon those people that we are guarding every side, and the first rustler of whom we catch a glimpse will be riddled."

Edward S. Ellis

"They are prepared for that, of course; be careful, friends, and don't expose yourselves more than you are obliged to, for there will be no let-up after the ball opens. I wish I could stay with you and help you out. I have been on the watch, ever since it grew dark, to steal off and make a run to the stockmen's camp, but I couldn't gain the first chance."

"I am afraid it is too late, anyway," said the captain, "for they are so far away that it will be over before they could arrive."

"Well, mother," said Fred, fearing that he was staying too long, "you and Jennie are ready, so let's go. Confound it! we must have a light for a few minutes; I know where there's a candle."

He ignited a match and quickly found a candle. This was lit and held above his head, so that he could look into the faces around him.

"There is no danger of their taking advantage of this until I leave," he explained, "and you can blow it out before that. I see you are there, mother; call Jennie down and let her join us."

"Jennie is not in the house!" was the reply, which fairly took away the breath of all.

CHAPTER XXXI

WHY IT WAS DONE

The yellow reflection of the candle lit up a group of wondering faces that were turned upon the mother, who stood in the middle of the room. Her countenance was pale, for she had passed through a great deal during the last half-hour, to say nothing of that which preceded it.

Before any one could frame the questions in his mind, she explains:

"I am not sure I have done right, but Jennie's departure was with my consent. She and I talked it over and discussed it in all its bearings, so far as we could see them, and she finally persuaded me that it was the right thing for her to do."

She paused, as if expecting some comment, but even Fred was silent; and still standing, with the candle held aloft, he kept his wondering gaze upon his parent.

"In the first place, Jennie convinced me that Monteith would only go to his own death by venturing out; at any rate, it would so result if he did not receive the signal from Mr. Vesey."

As she paused the amazed Sterry asked:

"But why did she think I would venture unless I got the sign from Vesey?"

"Because you told her so. You were so confident, when she expressed her misgivings, that you said you would wait a few minutes after 10 o'clock and then try it, even if no signal appeared."

"You are correct; I *did* tell her that."

"I consented to her plan on condition that if Mr. Vesey signalled you should go and she should stay; if he did not do so, she was to venture alone."

"Why didn't she consult with me?" asked Sterry; "I could have given her some suggestions."

"Ah, what a question, Mont!" said Fred Whitney, with a smile, as he comprehended the plan; "we know what suggestions you would have given her."

"True enough; she never would have made the attempt," he responded.

"And," said Mrs. Whitney, "your friend has not called to you."

"Which reminds me," exclaimed Sterry, stepping to the rear window and peering out. But everything in the direction of the stables was as dark and silent as the tomb.

"So you see that if you had followed the directions of Mr. Vesey," continued Mrs. Whitney, "no messenger would have left this place for the camp of the stockmen."

"I recall how closely she questioned me as to my idea of the course to take to reach the spot. I wanted to gain her confidence and told her everything, never suspecting that she entertained any such wild scheme."

"For which you cannot be blamed," remarked her brother; "but I don't understand how she expected to slip off unobserved."

"Nor do I," added Sterry, with a meaning glance at Capt. Asbury.

"I assure you I am innocent of complicity in the matter, for I would have opposed as strongly as any of you."

"It was that single difficulty which puzzled her," said the mother, "but Providence opened the way. While she stood trembling, with her cloak wrapped about her, Capt. Asbury called Monteith. I whispered to her 'Now!' and drew back the door. She stepped through, and was gone before any one, excepting myself, suspected anything."

"But what reason can she have for believing Vesey will favour her plan?" asked Sterry, feeling an admiration for the daring young woman. "He will be as much amazed as any one."

"The rustlers have notified us to leave the building, but have not said that they have a preference of one door over the other. If she finds herself confronted by strangers, she can easily explain who she is and say that her mother will soon join her. Can there be any objection to such a course, or is she likely to suffer on that account?"

Who could reply unfavourably to this question? The rustlers would simply conduct her to a place of safety, there to await the coming of her parent. Failure could bring no embarrassment to Jennie Whitney.

"The great difficulty, after all," remarked Capt. Asbury, "as it occurs to me, is that if your estimable daughter presents herself before Mr. Duke Vesey, he will refuse his help. What reason can she give that will induce him to aid her to pass beyond the camp?"

"I can think of none, but Jennie is hopeful that if she can see him alone he will permit her to do as she wishes."

"Does she contemplate walking the half-dozen miles or so to the camp of the cattlemen?" asked Sterry, in dismay.

"O, no; she expects to ride Mr. Sterry's mare."

"But—but—" stammered Monteith.

"She thought of all that," smiled the mother; "she took her saddle with her."

"Well, I'll be hanged if this isn't a little ahead of anything of which I ever heard or read!" was the only comment Monteith Sterry could make, as the full scheme unrolled before him.

"Jennie may fail," continued the proud parent, "but if she does, her situation and that of all of us will be no worse than before. If she fails, then you, too, Mr. Sterry, would have failed and lost your life without helping us."

"I am not prepared to admit that, but my part in the business seems to have passed beyond discussion."

Mrs. Whitney was about to continue her words when she ceased and faintly asked for a glass of water. Fred set down the candle and sprang to her help ahead of anyone, holding the glass, which was instantly brought, to her lips.

The poor woman had undergone great trials, as will be admitted, during the past few days. The excitement had sustained her until now something in the nature of a reaction came. Helping her to a chair, Fred affectionately fanned her, and did what he could to make her rally.

He was thus engaged when a second knock startled all. Capt. Asbury wheeled and demanded:

"Who's there?"

"Duke Vesey, under a flag of truce."

No name could have astonished the cattlemen more. This was the man whom Sterry had expected to meet, and in whose care it was supposed Jennie Whitney had placed herself.

Instead of that, he was asking admittance.

"Your flag will be respected," said Capt. Asbury, drawing back the bolts of the door, which was next swung inward a few inches.

The rustler stepped within, saying:

"I have been sent by Capt. Inman to inquire the meaning of the absence of Fred Whitney, who was sent here a considerable time ago."

"*That* is the cause of the delay," replied the captain, pointing to where the young rancher was doing his utmost to revive his mother.

The captain thought himself justified in turning the incident to account.

"She may not live more than half an hour. I suppose, under the circumstances, you folks won't vote to hang her son on his return, though it would be in keeping with your style of business."

"No; we leave that work to such as shoot down men before their homes, as was done last night. I didn't expect anything like this," he added more gently; "I will go back and report. I was told to bring the ladies, and as I can't take the elder just now, I suppose it's best to leave both till I learn what Capt. Inman wishes."

Monteith Sterry caught a significant glance of Vesey, while speaking, but was utterly unable to interpret it. He, however, removed to that side of the room, so as to place himself near him. Still the rustler made no other sign. Too many eyes were upon him.

One of Capt. Asbury's most noticeable points was his ability to "catch on" to a situation like the present. He saw the look given by the visitor, and translated it as meaning that he wished to make some communication to the other.

"Sterry," said the captain in his most rasping manner, "this is the fellow you were so tender on last night, and I suppose he will reciprocate when he gets a chance to draw a bead on you. I will leave to you the happiness of escorting him through the door, for the pleasure would quite overwhelm me."

"I am willing to act the gentleman at any time," replied Sterry, quickly seizing the opportunity of bringing himself near enough to hear what Vesey said without any one else noting it. As he was passing out the rustler remarked, in a quick undertone:

"I did my best, old fellow, but it won't work; they suspect something, and wouldn't let me go near the stable after dark. Sorry, but it's no use."

"But I thank you all the same," guardedly responded Sterry.

CHAPTER XXXII

THE HOSTAGE

Despite the alarm caused by the sudden illness of Mrs. Whitney, it was quickly apparent that nothing serious was the matter with her.

She had succumbed temporarily to the intense strain to which she had been subjected, and, under the considerate attention shown her, speedily rallied, declaring herself, within five minutes after the departure of Vesey, as well as ever.

"No one can rejoice more than I," observed Capt. Asbury; "and, since it is so trifling, you will not misunderstand me when I say that your illness seems to have been providential."

Fred and the rest looked inquiringly at the leader.

"The man who was here has gone back with the report of what he saw, and I think my words will cause him to represent the case—well," added the captain, with a smile, "as it appeared at that moment. That will secure further delay."

"But what can it all amount to?" asked Fred in turn; "they may give you a half-hour or so, but that does not count."

"If your estimable mother could manage to—ah—look desperately ill when the messenger returns, why, it might help matters."

But the good woman shook her head. Appreciating the gravity of the situation, she could not be a party to such a deception, even though beneficent results might follow.

"He saw me as I was, and thus he must see me when he comes again. My conscience would not permit it otherwise."

"You are right, Mrs. Whitney, and I beg your pardon," replied the captain.

Meanwhile, Monteith Sterry was thinking hard. Begging the indulgence of the others, he drew Capt. Asbury aside.

"I have decided upon an attempt," said he abruptly, "which you must not forbid, even though your judgment may condemn it."

"What is it?"

"I am going to try to get away."

"How?" was the surprised question; "what chance have you of succeeding, when every side of the house is watched?"

"Vesey told me, just as he was leaving, that he was not allowed to take his place as guard at the stables, which explains why he failed to give me the signal."

"He is unaware of what Miss Whitney has done?"

"I do not know of a surety, for he made no reference to it, but you heard his remark, which indicates that he is ignorant."

"Sterry," said the captain impressively, "the only friend you have among the rustlers is that same Vesey, and I place less faith in him than you do; yet you propose this wild scheme, without even the doubtful help of that man, and still expect me to approve it."

"You put it truthfully; I will only say that in the darkness I hope to be taken for one of them."

"And if you are?"

"I will work my way beyond the lines, and then make for the camp of the stockmen."

"On foot or horseback?"

"I can hardly expect to obtain a horse, but let me once gain the chance, and I will show some sprinting."

"You ignore the services of Miss Whitney?"

"It was a brave and characteristic deed, but a woman acts from intuition rather than reason. There is not a shadow of hope that she will accomplish anything."

"In my judgment, the prospect is as favourable for her as for you."

"Well," replied Sterry, "I rather expected you to talk that way, so your condemnation is discounted. I intend to pass out of the rear door within the next three minutes; I wish you to hold it, ready to open in the event of my deciding on a hasty return. If such return does not follow in the course of a quarter of an hour, you may conclude that I won't be back."

"I have already concluded that," was the significant comment.

The candle diffused enough illumination to show the anxious faces turned toward the couple as they walked back from the corner to which they had withdrawn for their brief consultation.

In the fewest words possible the captain explained the decision of the young man. He frankly stated that he did not believe there was any hope of success, but Sterry was firm in his resolution, and he would not interpose his authority. Fred Whitney was about to protest, but the expression of his friend's face showed that it would be useless, and he forebore.

Mont peered through the window, near the rear door, and, so far as he could judge, everything was favourable. Then he faced about, smiled, and without a word waved his friends good-by.

The door was drawn inward just enough to permit the passage of his body, and the next instant he had vanished.

Capt. Asbury sprang to the window and looked after him, but quick as he was, the time was sufficient for the youth to disappear as completely as though he were a dozen miles distant.

"If I may be allowed," said the captain, in his most suave manner, "I would suggest, Mr. Whitney, that you assist your mother to her apartment up stairs. She is in need of rest, and can obtain it there much better than here."

The good woman glanced suspiciously at the man, half

doubting the disinterestedness of his counsel, but he looked so grave and solicitous that she was sure she did him injustice. While she was hesitating, Fred added:

"It is good advice, mother; you can lie down, and when it is necessary I will call you. Come, please."

She could not decline, and the stalwart son, who seemed to have forgotten all about his wounded arm, almost carried her up the short stairs and to her room. He was so familiar with the interior that he needed no light, and deposited her as gently as an infant on the bed, kissed her an affectionate good-night, and promised to listen and come to her on hearing the slightest movement in her apartment.

"How does she seem to be?" asked Capt. Asbury, as Fred came down the stairs.

"As well as ever; but the little rest will be grateful. She has had enough to try the strongest person within the last few days."

"True indeed. I presume Vesey will soon be back with some ugly message from Inman and Cadmus, but we have delayed matters so long that I'm hopeful of keeping it up a while longer. Suppose, when this enterprising rustler shows himself, you allow me to do the talking, Fred. There is a good deal, you know, in the way you put things."

"I understand," replied the other, with a smile. "It will come, perhaps, more appropriately from you than me."

It was apparent from the manner of the captain that he felt considerable hope of success through the efforts of Miss Whitney or Sterry, or both. Time was the great factor. It would seem that three or four hours ought to bring the cattlemen, if either of the messengers succeeded in getting through the lines. While there was little doubt of the ability of the besieged being able to stand off their assailants for a much longer time, yet there was every reason to strain to the utmost the fortunate delay already secured.

A conflict was certain to result in a number of deaths to each side. Not only that, but it would intensify the bitterness already prevailing through many portions of Wyoming and Montana between the cowmen and rustlers, and postpone and increase the difficulty of the adjustment of the quarrel.

A full half-hour passed, during which the captain kept his place at the rear door, ready to admit Sterry should he make a dash for it. He did not appear, and when the fastenings of the structure were returned to their place the leader's heart was more hopeful than ever. He had just made a remark to that effect when a knocking was heard again on the front door, accompanied by Duke Vesey's announcement that it was himself who claimed admission.

The captain drew back the fastenings and the rustler stepped inside, his face showing great agitation.

"This is a fine state of things," he said, addressing young Whitney, Hawkridge and the captain.

"To what do you refer?" asked Whitney.

"You sent Mont Sterry out awhile ago, and the rustlers have caught him; he's in their hands and will be shot at daybreak. Capt. Inman sent me to you with that message, and to say that the fight will open in a few minutes. You can't play your tricks any longer on us."

It was apparent that Duke Vesey was in a rage over the

mishap that had befallen his friend.

Capt. Asbury quietly placed himself between the fellow and the door by which he had entered.

"What is the meaning of that?" demanded the rustler, turning his head; "I'm here under a flag of truce."

"Where is it? You haven't shown any, and you can't. I shall hold you as a hostage for the safety of Mont Sterry; whatever harm is visited upon *him* shall descend upon *your* head!"

CHAPTER XXXIII

THE PRISONER

It may be said that Monteith Sterry's main hope for the success of his perilous scheme lay in its boldness.

It was not to be supposed that the rustlers, surrounding the besieged on every hand, would forget the probability of just such an attempt as he made. The stockmen could not expect to slip away one by one, or in a body; nor was there anything to tempt such an effort, even if it offered a fair prospect of success; for, of necessity, they would have to depart on foot, and with the coming of daylight their situation would be worse than now, with a strong shelter above and around them.

But it was known among the defenders that two of their number were doomed, if they fell into the hands of the rustlers. It was probable, therefore, that one or both of these individuals would try to get away.

Whether or not the leaders held any distrust of Vesey cannot be known; but his little scheme for befriending Monteith Sterry was nipped in the bud by his being retained at the front of the building, where, as has been shown, he acted as the bearer of messages between Inman and Capt. Asbury.

Edward S. Ellis

There were men closely watching the building from the moment darkness closed over the scene. Had Sterry attempted to steal along the side of the house and then dodge away, he would have been detected and halted at once. On the contrary, he moved with his usual gait in a diagonal direction toward the stables. His object was to learn the likeliest method of leaving the place.

He had perhaps walked fifty feet, when some one advanced from the gloom and called, in an undertone:

"Halloo, who is that?"

"It's I, Smith; who are you?"

The name, of course, was a venture, but it was not uncommon, as the reader knows, and more likely to be right than any other. The best of it was, it seemed to satisfy the other, who, without announcing his own, asked:

"What are you doing?"

"I've been looking around to see what I could learn."

"Anything new?"

"No, not as far as I can discover; they seem to have a light burning in there, but are waiting for us."

"I wonder they didn't give you a shot; Vesey says they are desperate, and he brought back word that they would shoot the first of us seen prowling about the place. I wonder you didn't catch it."

"I took good care. When do you suppose the fight will open?"

"Pretty soon; I s'pose you are as tired of this dallying as the rest of us."

"Well, it strikes me as best to wait until sure everything is ready."

Sterry was anxious to end this pointless conversation, for the stranger had approached quite near and peered into his face, as though not free from suspicion. The darkness was deep, but on the other side of the ridge a small fire was burning, from fragments brought from the stables. Of this the adventurer meant to keep clear at all hazards. More than one rustler knew him intimately, and it might be that he to whom he was talking was an old acquaintance and enemy.

How Sterry longed for the presence of Vesey!

In a natural manner he sauntered up the ridge, as if his intention was to return to the camp-fire, that being the course most likely to dissipate any misgiving on the part of the other.

The latter made no response, and Sterry kept on, thinking:

"I'm rid of him, any way, and ought to have less trouble with others that may wish to ask questions."

But, glancing over his shoulder, he was startled to observe that the man, instead of moving off, as he had supposed, was standing motionless in the gloom, as if studying him.

"By gracious!" concluded the youth, "he must have noticed my voice, for, not knowing Smith, how could I imitate it?"

The situation would have made any one uneasy, but he did not hasten nor retard his footsteps until he reached the top of the ridge, and was able to observe the camp-fire clearly.

It was small, as has been said, but five or six figures were lolling about it, smoking, talking, and passing the dismal hours as inclination prompted. Other forms were moving hither and thither, some of them quite close to where Sterry had halted, though none paid him any attention.

The young man was looking for an opening by which he could make his way beyond the lines without attracting attention. The best prospect seemed to be the stretch of prairie extending from the front of the house toward the Big Horn Mountains.

"No one appears to be on the lookout there—"

At that instant each arm was tightly gripped, and the man with whom he had exchanged words but a few minutes before said:

"Mr. Smith, please go with us to the fire; my friend here is Smith, and he is the only one in our party with that name; maybe you are his double."

It was useless to resist, and Sterry replied:

"You know there are several Smiths in this country, and I ought to have the privilege of wearing the name without objection."

"We'll soon see," replied the first captor.

Within the next minute Sterry was marched in front of the camp-fire, where the full glare fell upon his countenance.

Then a howl of exultation went up, for more than half of the rustlers in the group recognized him.

CHAPTER XXXIV

OUT IN THE NIGHT

Enough has been already told for the reader to understand the scheme which Jennie Whitney, with the help of her mother, attempted to carry out for the benefit of the besieged cattlemen.

With her cloak around her shoulders and her saddle supported on one arm, she passed quickly from the rear of her home to the stables, only a short distance away. She had been on the alert for the signal of Duke Vesey, and, seeing it not, was prepared to encounter some one else.

In this she was not disappointed, for at the moment of catching sight of the dark mass where the horses were sheltered the figure of a man loomed into view as though he had risen from the ground. She stopped short, and observed, dimly, the forms of two others just behind him.

"Halloo!" exclaimed the nearest, "how is this?"

With peculiar emotions the young lady recognized the voice of Larch Cadmus. She hoped this was a favourable omen, and was quick to turn it to account.

"Larch, is that you?" she asked, peering forward as if uncertain of his identity.

"I declare, it is Miss Jennie!" he exclaimed, coming forward; "how is it you are alone?"

"Mother did not wish to come with me," replied the daughter, trying to avoid the necessity of direct deceit. "She will probably leave the house pretty soon."

The fellow was plainly embarrassed, despite the protecting gloom which concealed his features. Jennie knew him to be one of her most ardent admirers, though she had never liked him. Her hopes were now based upon making use of his regard for her.

"You have come out, Jennie, I suppose," said he, offering his hand, which she accepted, "so as not to be in the house when the—ah, trouble begins."

"O, I know it will be dreadful; I want to go as far away as I can—do you blame me, Larch?"

"Not at all—not at all; and I hope, Jennie, you don't blame me for all that your folks have suffered."

"Why, Larch, why should I blame you?" asked the young lady, coming fearfully near a fiction in making the query, for she knew many good reasons for censuring him in her heart. "But how soon do you intend—that is, how soon do the rest of your folks intend to attack the cowmen?"

"We—that is, they—expected to do so long ago, but there have been all sorts of delays; it will come pretty soon now."

"Where are you to place mother and me?"

"Over the ridge, yonder; you will be out of danger; you need fear nothing; why should you, for your mother will be with you and your brother will be with us, so that he can take no part in the fight."

He made no reference to Mont Sterry, and she was too wise to let fall a hint of her anxiety concerning him.

"But, Larch, suppose, when you set fire to the house, as I heard your folks intended, our people rush out and attack you?"

"Do they intend to do that?" he asked.

"I am sure I don't know; but you can see, if they do, the shooting will be going on all around mother and me."

"You can pass farther out on the plain or take shelter in the stable, among the horses."

"But that may be too late," interposed Jennie, in well-feigned alarm.

"You can take refuge here now."

"I can't bear to stay in the stable, for the horses will become terrified when the shooting begins; they may break loose and prove more dangerous than the flying bullets."

There was sense in this objection, and the rustler saw it. He was anxious to propitiate the young woman, whom he admired so ardently.

"Well, my dear, what would you like to do?"

"Now, Larch, you won't laugh at me if I tell you," she

Edward S. Ellis

replied, in her most coquettish manner.

"Laugh at you!" he protested; "this is no time for laughing; it was a shame that those people should turn your house into a fort, when it could do them no good. Tell me what you want and it shall be done, if it is in my power."

"Thanks! You are very kind, and I shall never forget this favour; I want to mount one of the best horses in the stable and ride out so far that I am sure to be beyond reach of danger."

The proposition staggered the rustler—so much so that it did not occur to him, just then, that the daughter appeared a great deal more anxious to look after her own safety than her mother's.

"You have a horse in the stable, haven't you?"

"Yes, Jack is there, and he is a splendid fellow; he is the one I want."

"But the saddle?"

"I have it with me; here it is; you and I will adjust it together."

And the impulsive miss placed the saddle in his grasp before he knew it. She certainly was rushing things. It must be admitted, too, that she showed fine discretion. There was but one way of handling Mr. Larch Cadmus, and she was using that way.

He turned about and walked to the door of the stable.

"Jack is in the second stall," she said, pausing at the entrance, "and his bridle is on the hook near his head."

The gloom was impenetrable, but a couple of matches gave Cadmus all the light needed, and a minute later he brought forth the fine animal, who whinnied with pleasure at recognizing his mistress, despite the gloom.

Jennie gave what help she could in saddling and bridling him, the other two men standing a little way off in silence. She kept up an incessant chatter, repeating her thanks to Cadmus for his kindness, and binding him more completely captive every minute.

But the rustler was inclined to be thoughtful, for before the animal was ready he began to feel misgivings as to the prudence of what he was doing. There was something odd, too, about the young lady mounting her pony, riding alone out on the plain, and leaving her mother behind. Then, too, she had emerged from the rear instead of the front of the house, as he judged from her line of approach.

Could there be any ulterior purpose in all this? If she would only cease her chatting for a minute or two he might figure out the problem, but the trouble was, nothing could stop her. In fact he didn't wish her to stop, for that voice was the most musical one to which he could listen, and he would have been glad had it sounded for hours in his ears.

He managed to drift dangerously near the truth.

"Can it be that she intends to ride away for help?" he reflected. "It has that look; but no, it is hardly that, for there isn't any help within reach that I know of. She might find it in the course of a day or two, but this affair will be over before daylight—I beg pardon, what was it you said, Jennie?"

"Why, Larch, I'm tempted to pull your ears; you are a fine gallant; here I have been standing full ten seconds, waiting for you to help me on the horse, and you have paid me no attention."

"It *was* rude, my dear; I hope you will pardon me," he replied, stepping quickly forward, "but I am very absent-minded to-night."

"I will pardon you, of course, for you have been so good and nice that it would be ungrateful for me to be impatient."

He took the Cinderella-like foot in his broad palm and cleverly assisted her in the saddle. While he helped to adjust the reins, her tongue rattled on harder than ever.

"How far, Larch, will it be necessary for me to ride so as to be sure—mind you, sure—of being out of the way when this awful business opens?"

"Well, I should say a hundred yards or so will be enough—"

"Mercy! do you think so? I ought to go two or three times as far as that; you won't object, will you? and when the shooting *does* begin, I can hurry Jack farther off."

"Do as you think best; but it seems to me, Jennie, that you are forgetting your mother—"

"O, no; when Fred brings her out—maybe he has done so now—tell her the direction I have gone and she will understand. Which is the best course for me to take? I guess it don't make any difference, so I will go this way."

Through all this apparently aimless chatter, Miss Jennie Whitney was using her wits. She knew a long ride was before her, and everything would be ruined if she lost her way. There was no moon or stars to give guidance, and she therefore carefully took her bearings while the chance was hers.

"I suppose it's all the same which course you follow, but I fear I am doing wrong in allowing you to ride off—"

"Now, don't spoil everything by regretting the handsome way in which you have indulged my whim; I think I will ride over the ridge to the left—"

"Hold on, Jennie, until I can speak to Inman; he may object—"

"You can speak to him after I am gone; good-night, Larch, and many thanks again for your kindness."

She rode off with her intelligent Jack on a walk until she was clear of the camp, when she touched him into an easy gallop.

Larch Cadmus stood looking into the gloom where she had vanished, almost before he comprehended her intention.

"Well, she's a puzzle!" he exclaimed to his two companions, who came forward; "I don't know what to make of her. What do you suppose she meant by that, boys?"

"It's easy enough to see," replied one of them, with a laugh; "she's gone off after help."

"Do you think so?" asked the startled Cadmus; "where can she get it?"

"She may bring back their hands."

Edward S. Ellis

"There are only two of them," said Larch, much relieved, "and they won't amount to anything in the rumpus. You don't imagine that she knows of any larger force anywhere in the neighbourhood?"

"She can't know of any, for there ain't any," was the clincher of the rustler; "or, if there is, she can't get it here in time to do Asbury and the rest any good."

Cadmus was relieved by the words of his friend. Enough misgivings, however, remained to make him say:

"There are so many moving about that her departure don't seem to be noticed; I'll take it as a favour if you don't mention it to any one, for now that she is gone I am sure I never should have allowed it."

The couple gave the promise, though their belief was that nothing serious would follow.

Leaving the two to keep watch at the stables, Cadmus sauntered to where Inman was seated near the camp-fire, smoking a pipe. A little inquiry disclosed that neither the leader nor any of his companions had noticed the departure of the young lady.

It was some time after this that Duke Vesey brought the report of Mrs. Whitney's illness as an explanation of her son's delay in returning to the camp of the rustlers.

Exasperated, and suspecting a pretense, Inman consented to a brief postponement of the attack.

The next startling occurrence was the capture of Monteith Sterry while trying to steal through the lines. As we have shown, he was identified the instant he was brought into the reflection of the firelight, and such precautions were taken that escape by him was out of the question.

When their impatience could stand it no longer, Vesey was sent to Capt. Asbury with the message which he delivered. Instead of his returning with a reply, Fred Whitney came back, bringing the announcement that Vesey had entered the house without claiming the protection of a truce, and after telling what he was directed to tell about Monteith Sterry, Capt. Asbury had directed Whitney to notify Capt. Inman that he would retain Vesey as a hostage, guaranteeing that whatever harm was visited upon Sterry should descend upon the head of Vesey.

This message, as may be supposed, caused consternation for some minutes in the camp of the rustlers. The feeling was quickly succeeded by exasperation. Had Inman and Cadmus been given the opportunity, no doubt they could have made a good argument to prove that, inasmuch as Vesey had passed back and forth several times after his first announcement of a flag of truce, and its acceptance by the besieged cowmen, it was not required by the law of nations that he should proclaim the fact while continuing to act as messenger between the hostiles.

On the other hand, the truth remained that he had entered the house of the rancher with weapons in his hands and without any claim of immunity from harm.

The question was such a nice one, capable of so many finely-drawn theories, that it is useless to discuss it here. Whatever decision we might reach, we could not feel assured we were right.

The hard fact confronted the rustlers that one of their principal men was in the power of the cowmen and was held as a hostage for the safety of the detested Monteith Sterry, who had been warned that he would be shot on sight by any rustler who gained the chance.

The unexpected phase of the situation caused a long and angry discussion between Capt. Ira Inman and his leaders, to which, as may be supposed, Fred Whitney and Monteith Sterry paid close attention.

CHAPTER XXXV

CONCLUSION

"Now, Jack, do your best, for everything depends on you."

Jennie Whitney looked around in the darkness and saw the glimmer of the rustlers' camp-fire, fully two hundred yards to the rear, with the shadowy figures moving to and fro.

"They may change their minds," she added, recalling the words of Larch Cadmus, "and decide to bring me back. Let them do it if they can!"

The intelligent pony acted as if he understood what was expected of him. With a light whinny at the pleasure he felt because of the opportunity of stretching out his beautiful limbs he broke into a swift canter, heading straight for the point where his rider believed the friendly camp was to be found.

She held the reins loose, knowing the danger of attempting to guide him where it was impossible to keep the points of the compass in mind. The way was smooth and even, although there is always danger in going at such speed in the night. She deemed the stake warranted it, however, and did not check the rapid pace.

Edward S. Ellis

Night on every hand and not a shining star overhead. If she could find the party of stockmen in time, so as to bring them back to her home, their strength would overawe the rustlers, and the whole difficulty could be arranged without the conflict which she looked upon with unspeakable dread.

"It will save him, too," she added, hesitating to pronounce the name that was in her heart, which would have throbbed more painfully had she known that in a brief while he would be helpless in the power of the men eager for his life. "I am glad he did not venture out of the house, when his friend could have done him no good. What will he think of me on learning what I have done? He will say that I am rash and foolish, and perhaps I am; will he suspect that it was to save him that I undertook this errand, which, after all, is attended with no risk to me worth mentioning?"

These were pleasant musings, but the task before her was too serious and made too close demands on her mental and physical energies for her to indulge in them. The delightful reverie could be deferred to a more convenient season.

Jennie Whitney had lived long enough in the West to understand that in times like the present it is safer to depend on the instinct of one's heart than upon one's reason. It seemed now and then that Jack was following the wrong direction, but she was wise in not interfering.

The gloom was so deep that she could see barely a few paces beyond the pointed ears in front, but when the ground showed an abrupt rise she recalled the location and knew he had followed the exact course she desired.

She pulled slightly on the reins and he dropped to a walk. At the same moment something dark moved aside, the pony diverting his own steps to avoid it. She experienced a slight shock of fright, but recognized the object as one of the cattle probably belonging to their own herd. Others showed dimly here and there as the horse carefully picked his way forward.

"Halloo, who's that?" called a gruff voice from the darkness, the hail proving more startling than the first surprise.

"It is I, Jennie Whitney," replied the young lady, "and I am searching for help."

"Well, I'll be hanged! What's up, Miss Jennie?"

It was Budd Hankinson who came forward on foot, his figure appearing of gigantic proportions in the gloom. He was more alarmed than she, as he had warrant for being, knowing, as he did, that some extraordinary cause must have brought the girl to this place alone at that hour of the night.

She quickly told her story, explaining that Fred was held a prisoner by the rustlers, else he would have hastened back to secure the assistance for which she was looking.

"You're a brave girl," said the honest fellow, as he laid his hand on the reins of the pony; "there are mighty few that would have done what you've done to-night."

"Never mind about that, Budd, but tell me what to do."

"Why, you mustn't do anything; I'll do the rest."

"No, you may help me, but what is it to be?"

"Luck's running your way, Jennie; the stockmen have moved their camp since Fred left this morning."

"Mercy! I thought I had only two or three miles farther to go."

"Their camp isn't more'n half a mile off, right over the swell yonder; we'll be there in a jiffy."

"And you will go with me?"

"Wal, I reckon; what sort of a chap do you take me for?"

"Where is Weber?"

"Three miles to the south, which is in t'other direction; we won't have time to look him up, and it wouldn't do any good if we did. We made a change of grazing grounds, as I s'pose Fred told you, but some of the cattle strayed off here and I was looking 'em up when I heard your pony."

"Where's your horse?"

"Not far; wait here and I'll be right back."

He was gone but a few minutes, when he returned in the saddle.

"It won't do to go too fast," he explained, moving forward with his animal on a walk, "but we can keep beside each other."

Riding thus carefully, he questioned her about the stirring incidents at the house, and she gave him the particulars. The sagacious fellow had seen before this how matters stood between her and Monteith Sterry, and he knew her anxiety, but his good taste prevented any reference to it further than to say:

"I hope Mont will be too wise to try to slip out of the house, for if he does he's sure to be grabbed up by them, and they won't give him a chance for his life."

"Do you think he will make the attempt, Budd?"

"No, now that he knows you have started, for you've got a mighty sight better chance to succeed than he could have. Of course he has too much sense for anything of the kind."

It was well that neither of them suspected the truth.

"There they are!"

They had reached the top of the elevation, and saw before them the twinkling lights of several camp-fires. The stockmen, fully understanding the nature of the work they had undertaken, conducted themselves like a force invading a hostile country. Regular sentinels were stationed, to prevent the insidious approach of an enemy.

The couple rode down the hill, and, as they expected, were challenged on the edge of the camp. Inasmuch as Budd had visited the men during the day and formed numerous acquaintances, he had little difficulty in making himself known. All, excepting the guards, had retired for the night, but the visitor was conducted to the place where Maj. Sitgraves was asleep, Jennie remaining on the outskirts with one of the sentinels, who treated her with all courtesy.

Maj. Sitgraves was a brave man, who had only to hear the story brought to him by the honest cowboy to understand the urgency of the case. It was now near midnight, and the attack at the ranch was liable to be made at any moment. The stockmen could not reach the scene of danger too soon.

Almost instantly the camp was astir. It looked as if the men had received orders to attack a force of Indians, whose location was just made known to them, and, in point of fact, the situation was somewhat similar, for a brisk fight appeared inevitable. Three rustlers whom the major was particularly anxious to arrest were Ira Inman, Larch Cadmus and Duke Vesey, and he especially wanted the first two. They were with the party not far off, and, aside from the call for help of the imperilled stockmen, the prospect of capturing those fellows was sufficient warrant for a prompt movement.

Within half an hour after Jennie Whitney's meeting with Budd Hankinson the party of half a hundred were galloping westward, she riding at the head, with Maj. Sitgraves and Budd, who acted as guide to the expedition.

Hope arose with every rod advanced, for if fighting had begun the reports of the guns would be heard, but the listening ears failed to catch the first hostile sound from the Whitney ranch. By and by a point was reached which would have shown them the flash of the guns, but the gloom remained impenetrable.

The twinkling camp-fire, at the base of the ridge, gave just the guidance needed, and, with Budd Hankinson's intimate knowledge of the country, enabled the force to tell exactly where they were.

Maj. Sitgraves decided to defer his attack until daylight, unless the safety of the beleaguered cattlemen should force him to assault sooner. In the darkness, with the open country around, and the excellent animals at the command of the rustlers, most of them would escape upon learning the strength of the assailants. At the earliest dawn the stockmen could be so placed that, as the commander believed, nearly if not quite all of the law-breakers would be corralled.

Accordingly, a halt was made while yet a considerable way off, and Budd Hankinson went forward on foot to reconnoitre. Upon his report must depend the action of the stockmen.

The fellow was gone more than three-quarters of an hour, and when he came back he brought astounding news.

Not a solitary rustler was to be found anywhere near the ranch.

Hardly able to credit the fact, Budd picked his way to the building, knocked, and was admitted. There the amazing truth was made known. Capt. Ira Inman and all his men had been gone for an hour, and were probably miles distant at that moment.

The detention of Duke Vesey as a hostage for the safety of Monteith Sterry proved the key to the whole situation. When Inman learned how he had been outwitted he was enraged to the point of ordering an attack at once, with the resolve to give mercy to no one. He even threatened to visit his fury upon Fred Whitney, who had shown such punctilious regard for his parole, for it would seem that under the circumstances he would have been warranted in staying behind with his friends.

But before taking so rash a step, the cooler judgment of the leader came to his rescue—He placed a high value on Duke Vesey, who had been associated with him in several dangerous enterprises, and he knew that any harm done to Sterry would recoil on him, just as the grim Capt. Asbury had threatened.

After prolonged discussion with Cadmus and others, it was decided to offer to exchange Sterry for Vesey. The proposition was accepted, and the exchange faithfully made, though considerable more delay was involved.

But while it was under way Inman learned of Jennie Whitney's flight toward the Big Horn Mountains. Keener of wit than Larch Cadmus, he suspected the truth at once, though he knew nothing of the proximity of the stockmen.

Before making the attack and attempt to burn the building he sent out two of his best mounted men in the direction taken by her, to investigate. They did so with such skill that neither Budd Hankinson nor any of the stockmen suspected them. They returned with news of the approach of a body too powerful for them to think of combating. They therefore fled in the darkness, the promptness of the leaders probably hastened by the knowledge that they were the parties for whom the stockmen were looking.

And so ended the campaign. The situation had been critical for a long time, and there were moments, time and again, when the most trifling incident intervened to avert a fearful conflict between men of the same race and blood; but all had now passed, and it may be said that not so much as a hostile shot had been exchanged.

The main events of the troubles in Wyoming between the cowmen and rustlers are too well remembered to require recital at our hands. The expedition referred to in another place left Cheyenne in April for Nolan's Ranch, a hundred or more miles distant. Within the following month, the Sixth U.S. Cavalry brought all of them back to Cheyenne as prisoners of war, thus saving them from extermination at the hands of the indignant rustlers, who had them hemmed in on all sides.

Fred Whitney sold out his ranch, near the headwaters of Powder River, and moved eastward. He was not actuated by fear, for it will be conceded that he proved his courage, but he desired to take his loved mother and sister away from the sorrowful memories that must always cling to the place.

It will not surprise the reader to learn, further, that Monteith Sterry found it quite convenient to make his home in the same neighborhood with the Whitneys, and it was but a short time after this removal eastward that a most pleasing incident occurred in the lives of the young man and Miss Whitney, of the nature of which we are sure the reader does not need to be told.

Choose from Thousands of 1stWorldLibrary Classics By

A. M. Barnard
Ada Leverson
Adolphus William Ward
Aesop
Agatha Christie
Alexander Aaronsohn
Alexander Kielland
Alexandre Dumas
Alfred Gatty
Alfred Ollivant
Alice Duer Miller
Alice Turner Curtis
Alice Dunbar
Allen Chapman
Alleyne Ireland
Ambrose Bierce
Amelia E. Barr
Amory H. Bradford
Andrew Lang
Andrew McFarland Davis
Andy Adams
Angela Brazil
Anna Alice Chapin
Anna Sewell
Annie Besant
Annie Hamilton Donnell
Annie Payson Call
Annie Roe Carr
Annonaymous
Anton Chekhov
Archibald Lee Fletcher
Arnold Bennett
Arthur C. Benson
Arthur Conan Doyle
Arthur M. Winfield
Arthur Ransome
Arthur Schnitzler
Arthur Train
Atticus
B.H. Baden-Powell
B. M. Bower
B. C. Chatterjee
Baroness Emmuska Orczy
Baroness Orczy
Basil King
Bayard Taylor
Ben Macomber
Bertha Muzzy Bower
Bjornstjerne Bjornson

Booth Tarkington
Boyd Cable
Bram Stoker
C. Collodi
C. E. Orr
C. M. Ingleby
Carolyn Wells
Catherine Parr Traill
Charles A. Eastman
Charles Amory Beach
Charles Dickens
Charles Dudley Warner
Charles Farrar Browne
Charles Ives
Charles Kingsley
Charles Klein
Charles Hanson Towne
Charles Lathrop Pack
Charles Romyn Dake
Charles Whibley
Charles Willing Beale
Charlotte M. Braeme
Charlotte M. Yonge
Charlotte Perkins Stetson
Clair W. Hayes
Clarence Day Jr.
Clarence E. Mulford
Clemence Housman
Confucius
Coningsby Dawson
Cornelis DeWitt Wilcox
Cyril Burleigh
D. H. Lawrence
Daniel Defoe
David Garnett
Dinah Craik
Don Carlos Janes
Donald Keyhoe
Dorothy Kilner
Dougan Clark
Douglas Fairbanks
E. Nesbit
E. P. Roe
E. Phillips Oppenheim
E. S. Brooks
Earl Barnes
Edgar Rice Burroughs
Edith Van Dyne
Edith Wharton

Edward Everett Hale
Edward J. O'Biren
Edward S. Ellis
Edwin L. Arnold
Eleanor Atkins
Eleanor Hallowell Abbott
Eliot Gregory
Elizabeth Gaskell
Elizabeth McCracken
Elizabeth Von Arnim
Ellem Key
Emerson Hough
Emilie F. Carlen
Emily Bronte
Emily Dickinson
Enid Bagnold
Enilor Macartney Lane
Erasmus W. Jones
Ernie Howard Pie
Ethel May Dell
Ethel Turner
Ethel Watts Mumford
Eugene Sue
Eugenie Foa
Eugene Wood
Eustace Hale Ball
Evelyn Everett-green
Everard Cotes
F. H. Cheley
F. J. Cross
F. Marion Crawford
Fannie E. Newberry
Federick Austin Ogg
Ferdinand Ossendowski
Fergus Hume
Florence A. Kilpatrick
Fremont B. Deering
Francis Bacon
Francis Darwin
Frances Hodgson Burnett
Frances Parkinson Keyes
Frank Gee Patchin
Frank Harris
Frank Jewett Mather
Frank L. Packard
Frank V. Webster
Frederic Stewart Isham
Frederick Trevor Hill
Frederick Winslow Taylor

Friedrich Kerst
Friedrich Nietzsche
Fyodor Dostoyevsky
G.A. Henty
G.K. Chesterton
Gabrielle E. Jackson
Garrett P. Serviss
Gaston Leroux
George A. Warren
George Ade
Geroge Bernard Shaw
George Cary Eggleston
George Durston
George Ebers
George Eliot
George Gissing
George MacDonald
George Meredith
George Orwell
George Sylvester Viereck
George Tucker
George W. Cable
George Wharton James
Gertrude Atherton
Gordon Casserly
Grace E. King
Grace Gallatin
Grace Greenwood
Grant Allen
Guillermo A. Sherwell
Gulielma Zollinger
Gustav Flaubert
H. A. Cody
H. B. Irving
H.C. Bailey
H. G. Wells
H. H. Munro
H. Irving Hancock
H. R. Naylor
H. Rider Haggard
H. W. C. Davis
Haldeman Julius
Hall Caine
Hamilton Wright Mabie
Hans Christian Andersen
Harold Avery
Harold McGrath
Harriet Beecher Stowe
Harry Castlemon
Harry Coghill
Harry Houidini

Hayden Carruth
Helent Hunt Jackson
Helen Nicolay
Hendrik Conscience
Hendy David Thoreau
Henri Barbusse
Henrik Ibsen
Henry Adams
Henry Ford
Henry Frost
Henry James
Henry Jones Ford
Henry Seton Merriman
Henry W Longfellow
Herbert A. Giles
Herbert Carter
Herbert N. Casson
Herman Hesse
Hildegard G. Frey
Homer
Honore De Balzac
Horace B. Day
Horace Walpole
Horatio Alger Jr.
Howard Pyle
Howard R. Garis
Hugh Lofting
Hugh Walpole
Humphry Ward
Ian Maclaren
Inez Haynes Gillmore
Irving Bacheller
Isabel Cecilia Williams
Isabel Hornibrook
Israel Abrahams
Ivan Turgenev
J.G.Austin
J. Henri Fabre
J. M. Barrie
J. M. Walsh
J. Macdonald Oxley
J. R. Miller
J. S. Fletcher
J. S. Knowles
J. Storer Clouston
J. W. Duffield
Jack London
Jacob Abbott
James Allen
James Andrews
James Baldwin

James Branch Cabell
James DeMille
James Joyce
James Lane Allen
James Lane Allen
James Oliver Curwood
James Oppenheim
James Otis
James R. Driscoll
Jane Abbott
Jane Austen
Jane L. Stewart
Janet Aldridge
Jens Peter Jacobsen
Jerome K. Jerome
Jessie Graham Flower
John Buchan
John Burroughs
John Cournos
John F. Kennedy
John Gay
John Glasworthy
John Habberton
John Joy Bell
John Kendrick Bangs
John Milton
John Philip Sousa
John Taintor Foote
Jonas Lauritz Idemil Lie
Jonathan Swift
Joseph A. Altsheler
Joseph Carey
Joseph Conrad
Joseph E. Badger Jr
Joseph Hergesheimer
Joseph Jacobs
Jules Vernes
Julian Hawthrone
Julie A Lippmann
Justin Huntly McCarthy
Kakuzo Okakura
Karle Wilson Baker
Kate Chopin
Kenneth Grahame
Kenneth McGaffey
Kate Langley Bosher
Kate Langley Bosher
Katherine Cecil Thurston
Katherine Stokes
L. A. Abbot
L. T. Meade

L. Frank Baum
Latta Griswold
Laura Dent Crane
Laura Lee Hope
Laurence Housman
Lawrence Beasley
Leo Tolstoy
Leonid Andreyev
Lewis Carroll
Lewis Sperry Chafer
Lilian Bell
Lloyd Osbourne
Louis Hughes
Louis Joseph Vance
Louis Tracy
Louisa May Alcott
Lucy Fitch Perkins
Lucy Maud Montgomery
Luther Benson
Lydia Miller Middleton
Lyndon Orr
M. Corvus
M. H. Adams
Margaret E. Sangster
Margret Howth
Margaret Vandercook
Margaret W. Hungerford
Margret Penrose
Maria Edgeworth
Maria Thompson Daviess
Mariano Azuela
Marion Polk Angellotti
Mark Overton
Mark Twain
Mary Austin
Mary Catherine Crowley
Mary Cole
Mary Hastings Bradley
Mary Roberts Rinehart
Mary Rowlandson
M. Wollstonecraft Shelley
Maud Lindsay
Max Beerbohm
Myra Kelly
Nathaniel Hawthrone
Nicolo Machiavelli
O. F. Walton
Oscar Wilde

Owen Johnson
P.G. Wodehouse
Paul and Mabel Thorne
Paul G. Tomlinson
Paul Severing
Percy Brebner
Percy Keese Fitzhugh
Peter B. Kyne
Plato
Quincy Allen
R. Derby Holmes
R. L. Stevenson
R. S. Ball
Rabindranath Tagore
Rahul Alvares
Ralph Bonehill
Ralph Henry Barbour
Ralph Victor
Ralph Waldo Emmerson
Rene Descartes
Ray Cummings
Rex Beach
Rex E. Beach
Richard Harding Davis
Richard Jefferies
Richard Le Gallienne
Robert Barr
Robert Frost
Robert Gordon Anderson
Robert L. Drake
Robert Lansing
Robert Lynd
Robert Michael Ballantyne
Robert W. Chambers
Rosa Nouchette Carey
Rudyard Kipling
Saint Augustine
Samuel B. Allison
Samuel Hopkins Adams
Sarah Bernhardt
Sarah C. Hallowell
Selma Lagerlof
Sherwood Anderson
Sigmund Freud
Standish O'Grady
Stanley Weyman
Stella Benson
Stella M. Francis

Stephen Crane
Stewart Edward White
Stijn Streuvels
Swami Abhedananda
Swami Parmananda
T. S. Ackland
T. S. Arthur
The Princess Der Ling
Thomas A. Janvier
Thomas A Kempis
Thomas Anderton
Thomas Bailey Aldrich
Thomas Bulfinch
Thomas De Quincey
Thomas Dixon
Thomas H. Huxley
Thomas Hardy
Thomas More
Thornton W. Burgess
U. S. Grant
Upton Sinclair
Valentine Williams
Various Authors
Vaughan Kester
Victor Appleton
Victor G. Durham
Victoria Cross
Virginia Woolf
Wadsworth Camp
Walter Camp
Walter Scott
Washington Irving
Wilbur Lawton
Wilkie Collins
Willa Cather
Willard F. Baker
William Dean Howells
William le Queux
W. Makepeace Thackeray
William W. Walter
William Shakespeare
Winston Churchill
Yei Theodora Ozaki
Yogi Ramacharaka
Young E. Allison
Zane Grey

www.ingramcontent.com/pod-product-compliance
Lightning Source LLC
Chambersburg PA
CBHW050736180626
46814CB00002B/787